essentials

Family Law

ASPEN PUBLISHERS

essentials

Family Law

Katharine K. Baker
Chicago-Kent College of Law

Katharine B. Silbaugh
Boston University of Law School

Wolters Kluwer
Law & Business

AUSTIN   BOSTON   CHICAGO   NEW YORK   THE NETHERLANDS

Aspen Publishers
Attn: Permissions Department
76 Ninth Avenue, 7th Floor
New York, NY 10011-5201

To contact Customer Care, e-mail customer.care@aspenpublishers.com, call 1-800-234-1660, fax 1-800-901-9075, or mail correspondence to:

Aspen Publishers
Attn: Order Department
PO Box 990
Frederick, MD 21705

Printed in the United States of America.

1 2 3 4 5 6 7 8 9 0

ISBN 978-0-7355-8296-5

Library of Congress Cataloging-in-Publication Data

Baker, Katharine K., 1962–
    Family law: the essentials / Katharine K. Baker, Katharine B. Silbaugh. — 1st ed.
        p. cm.
    ISBN-13: 978-0-7355-8296-5
    ISBN-10: 0-7355-8296-3
1. Domestic relations — United States.   I. Silbaugh, Katharine B. II. Title.

KF505.B35 2009
346.7301'5 — dc22

                                                                                2009013016

About Wolters Kluwer Law & Business

Wolters Kluwer Law & Business is a leading provider of research information and workflow solutions in key specialty areas. The strengths of the individual brands of Aspen Publishers, CCH, Kluwer Law International and Loislaw are aligned within Wolters Kluwer Law & Business to provide comprehensive, in-depth solutions and expert-authored content for the legal, professional and education markets.

CCH was founded in 1913 and has served more than four generations of business professionals and their clients. The CCH products in the Wolters Kluwer Law & Business group are highly regarded electronic and print resources for legal, securities, antitrust and trade regulation, government contracting, banking, pension, payroll, employment and labor, and healthcare reimbursement and compliance professionals.

Aspen Publishers is a leading information provider for attorneys, business professionals and law students. Written by preeminent authorities, Aspen products offer analytical and practical information in a range of specialty practice areas from securities law and intellectual property to mergers and acquisitions and pension/benefits. Aspen's trusted legal education resources provide professors and students with high-quality, up-to-date and effective resources for successful instruction and study in all areas of the law.

Kluwer Law International supplies the global business community with comprehensive English-language international legal information. Legal practitioners, corporate counsel and business executives around the world rely on the Kluwer Law International journals, loose-leafs, books and electronic products for authoritative information in many areas of international legal practice.

Loislaw is a premier provider of digitized legal content to small law firm practitioners of various specializations. Loislaw provides attorneys with the ability to quickly and efficiently find the necessary legal information they need, when and where they need it, by facilitating access to primary law as well as state-specific law, records, forms and treatises.

Wolters Kluwer Law & Business, a unit of Wolters Kluwer, is headquartered in New York and Riverwoods, Illinois. Wolters Kluwer is a leading multinational publisher and information services company.

For Jane, William, Duncan, and Daniel, without whom this
would have been quick and cheerless
K.S.

For KEB and GPB, who stubbornly, if lovingly, insist that
family matters
K.B.

Table of Contents

CHAPTER 5

Conclusion   181

ᔓ 1 ᔕ

Introduction

Families are a product of individual decisions and declarations, legal rules, social understandings, cultural practices and constraints, religious expectations, intimate behavior, and economies. This book is about the way law shapes families, and the way law responds to social, cultural, religious, and economic transformations in family practices. It covers the practical aspects of legal regulation of families, as well as the history, economics, and culture that both shape and confound legal regulation of family relationships.

A definition of *family* might be useful to this task. Unfortunately, we cannot provide a comprehensive definition without begging further questions. There are a variety of interpersonal relationships understood by some or many as familial. Some people have an understanding of family as coterminous with the law, while others view the legal role as more peripheral to the meaning of family. On southern plantations in the eighteenth and nineteenth centuries, enslaved adults did not have access to legal marriage. To communicate their union to each other and their community, a man and a woman would jump over a broom in the presence of others. On some understandings, but not others, jumping the broom made them family. Children born to that woman, even if those children were conceived involuntary with the man who had enslaved her, will also test the meaning of family.

Today, some people call a heterosexual couple that has lived together for years, had regular sexual relations, and shared emotional and material resources a family. Some people say the same thing about same-sex couples. Others do not. Family may at times have a provable objective quality, but it is also a subjective sense of connection. We will see that the objective and subjective meanings inform each other.

When thinking about children, some people start with a biologically-based notion of family. Many people refer to the genetic father of a child as the *real* father, even though the law does not necessarily consider him family. On the other hand, countless people grow up calling adults who are not legally or genetically related to them "aunt" or "uncle," because they view them as family.

People often experience families as a web of connections that sits between individuals and communities. At times families have been primarily embedded in communities. Marriages were created by obligations among extended families rather than affections between individuals, and marriage led to new obligations to extended families. In the modern era, a more individualistic model of families has emerged to compete with the community-based model. In the individualistic model, the family is composed of a finite group of two adults and their dependents, and entry and exit involves a large measure of individual freedom, without accounting for the impact on a community beyond the household. Nonetheless, family is often experienced as a mini-community, situated in a larger one.

Perhaps a family consists of a group of people who share intense emotional bonds and who develop emotional and material interdependencies and obligations. But some families have minimal emotional connection, and many emotional interdependencies can develop in relationships that people do not view as familial. Meanwhile, material interdependencies are a common aspect of many commercial contracts.

The concept of family also changes over time and depends on the context. Families are perceived at times as a moral and cultural institution, the value of which is primarily symbolic. At other times they may be perceived as an economic institution or one that is practical in some other way, such as providing stability in the population. Cultural changes in notions of individuality are reflected in family practices, as when the rise of companionate marriage displaced arranged marriage. Changing notions of equality are reflected in personal and legal understandings of marriage. In addition, changes in family practices and conceptions are sometimes created by technological advances. For example, the advent of reliable birth control separated sex within and outside marriage from pregnancy and childbirth. The availability of genetic testing challenged notions of paternity. The understanding and boundary of family have been as contested over time as they are today, but different controversies destabilized what each generation saw as the new stability. Fixed but accurate definitions of *family* are not practical.

Perhaps we could provide a definition of *family law*, even if we cannot comprehensively define *family*. That does not turn out to be uncontested, either, but we can present some alternatives. Most people do not form family ties because of their legal incidents, or even with an accurate awareness of the legal consequences. The law shadows family life, as a largely unnoticed attribute of the everyday experience of families.

Many family lawyers, also called *domestic relations lawyers*, view family law as the legal rules around a set of topics, primarily divorce, child custody and support, and adoption. But family law may be any law that responds to a group of individuals who define themselves as a family, rather than as individuals. On this measure, family law includes the traditional legal interventions of marriage, adoption, divorce, property distribution, alimony or maintenance, child custody, child support, and trust and estate law. But it also includes background legal principles, usually from contract and property, that fill in when a set of individuals functions as a family. Family law can include the law of child protective services (abuse and neglect), as well as laws of general applicability that include special rules for families, such as tax and Social Security law, immigration law, employment law, banking, bankruptcy, and real estate law. The family lawyer needs familiarity with tax, credit, bankruptcy, and estate law, as well as the more central law of family dissolution, in order to effectively represent her clients. In this book we focus on the traditional topics of family law, reminding the reader occasionally of the additional laws of general applicability that treat families as a group rather than as individuals.

A few characteristics of family law are worth overview at the outset. The first is the role of discretion. Many standards in family law — that things should be divided "equitably" or that custody should be determined "in the best interest of the child" — are particularly abstract. Practices and standards do develop, but most inquiries are fact intensive. Predictable outcomes for some subjects, such as alimony and child custody, aren't available. That discretion can affect the strategy of litigants, who cannot accurately predict results and therefore can have difficulty managing settlement discussions. The absence of clear rules also deviates from the basic premise that the law should apply evenly to all who are similarly situated.

When standards are discretionary, judges often appreciate any guidance they can obtain. In that light, expert testimony can become incredibly important to the outcome of a case. But experts on emotional matters — psychologists and psychiatrists — aren't trained in applying legal principles evenhandedly. Experts may bring biases to their recommendations that would not be permitted to influence a legal proceeding were they articulated. Examples might include a view that the wealthier household is better or that the mother-daughter bond is more important than the father-daughter bond.

Nonetheless, judges often believe that the ability of these experts to evaluate a family is superior to their own and can be quite deferential to the findings of experts when applying highly discretionary standards. Experts may also investigate using tools that judges lack from the bench, which can help the experts reach an informed result. But given their determinative role in many cases, it should be a cause of some concern that experts are not bound by due process norms in applying standards that bind the judge who accepts their recommendation.

In this chapter we introduce the themes and conundrums that manifest themselves when the law recognizes and regulates families. These themes help to explain what the law attempts to achieve, and what it avoids. Family law often differs both from what people believe it is, and from what they think it should be. This reflects the absence of societal consensus on what family law should do. It also reflects disagreement over how to achieve the goals of family law upon which we do agree.

We provide an overview of family law, but we do not vouch for the law's coherence. There is not an entirely reliable map of the field, although we will explain some guideposts. This body of law is tasked with a thankless mission: Impose legal principles and notions of justice onto relationships that most people relate to as outside the law. The stubbornness of that task generates the following themes.

A. RECURRING THEMES

1. The Centrality of Marriage and Its Multiple Meanings

The focal point of the legal response to adult relationships remains marriage. Marriage has far-reaching legal consequences that cross many areas of a person's legal identity: it confers health-care decision-making authority, it changes how individuals own property, it subjects individuals to a different criminal law regime, and it changes a person's tax obligations, to name just a few of the hundreds of legal consequences of marriage. Given these legal consequences, it is accurate to call marriage a legal institution.

At the same time, marriage cannot be described as only a legal institution because it has an extensive and impressive history of meaning within religions and cultures that falls outside of the current reach we ascribe to legal institutions. It seems likely that people are drawn to marriage for reasons other than its legal consequences. Some would argue it is entirely a cultural and religious entity to which government then attaches legal consequences. Others would argue that marriage is primarily a legal institution and status. Marriage must be both, because neither the cultural nor the legal can thrive without the other.

The two aspects of marriage, legal and cultural, aren't easily disentangled by legal actors; in many cases they cannot be. Their roots are intertwined. Marriage was originally regulated by religious and customary institutions in many cultures, but at a time when religious and customary institutions looked and felt like what we call law today. In early Western history, marriage was a local, barely regulated institution, if indeed it could be called an institution at all. The evidence we have suggests that customs varied widely. Temporary pair-bonding for the purpose of producing children is as old as humanity, but whether that pair-bonding was understood as a social arrangement that we might recognize as a kind of marriage is a different question.

At the beginning of the first millennium, as the Catholic Church expanded its influence throughout Europe, it took control of marriage. Motivated probably by a desire to assert control over family formation and reproduction, and careful to incorporate different local customs for fear of driving people away, the church began to define *marriage* as a sacred institution, one that was sanctioned by God and a necessary part of most pious lives. Because it was a sacred institution, the church was able to prescribe its critical components. Thus, the church decided who could marry (one unmarried man and one unmarried woman), what was necessary to marry (the presence of a priest, except in extraordinary circumstances), and what it meant to be married (a lifelong union for the purpose of rearing children). Children born outside of marriage were illegitimate, a highly disadvantageous legal and cultural status.

Viewed from an economic perspective, though, marriage at this time was not just the locus of reproduction, as the church maintained, but a locus of production. In an overwhelming agrarian society, marriage delineated economic units that were responsible for their own survival. Households usually consumed only what they produced and did not produce much more than they consumed. In these units, both men and women provided for the household, and both took responsibility for children. What kind of services they provided and which kind of child-care responsibilities they assumed were often gendered (men did some things and women did others), but both genders were considered an essential part of a well-functioning, economically productive household.

The sixteenth through the early nineteenth centuries marked the emergence of two important trends for families and family law. First, growing urbanization meant that more and more work was being done away from the household, more often by men in many industries, although certain industries employed large numbers of women and children. Men began to earn money, while women were far less likely to do so. Homes came to be seen less as units of production and more as units of reproduction. By the twentieth century, homes would be viewed as units of reproduction and of consumption, the latter role assigned predominantly to women. Second, the church's power throughout Europe waned as secular governments grew in influence. These governments began to assert some control over marriage.

To this day, religious and secular authorities continue to share authority over marriage, and there is still, as their always has been, some cultural understanding of marriage that is not explicitly either religious or legal. This shared authority over the definition and understanding of marriage, between cultural, religious, and legal institutions, informs the meaning of marriage. At times, it also presents dilemmas to courts and legislators, who may not be sure of the boundaries of their legitimate role in shaping marriage.

Family law scholars have developed a number of ways of describing the operation and purpose of marriage. These different models are sometimes offered to explain legal doctrine or social practices. Each model does a good job of explaining some social or legal practices, while falling short of describing other ones. While none is definitive, the family law student will find familiarity with some of these theoretical debates about marriage helpful. The dominant theories of marriage include status, contract, economic, religious, partnership, companionate, and procreation/reproduction.

Status.   An early Supreme Court case suggested that marriage was a contract between a man, a woman, and the state.[1] When the state is a party to the relationship, we think of the institution as a *status*. The marriage contract derives its meaning from a somewhat stable public institution and is defined by the state as third party. The state, in this model, develops the legal consequences of marriage, and while couples consent to enter the marriage, they do not themselves create its meaning through contractual negotiations. Rather, they accept the status as defined by the state. The status notion of marriage can be understood as a cultural phenomenon as well as a legal one: Couples may live privately and negotiate the terms of their relationship without marrying, but when they decide to marry, they are opting for inclusion in a public institution that has meaning derived and controlled by the larger culture, not the parties to the marriage.

Contract.   By contrast, many view marriage as a fundamentally private contract between individuals. Promises are exchanged, and the law seeks to untangle the nature of those promises and to the best of its ability understand and enforce the promises or provide adequate remedies when promises are broken. On this theory, the many legal conditions that make up marriage are in the nature of default terms in a contract, filling in the gaps of negotiation with common wisdom and practice but allowing for individual tailoring when couples deviate from the norm. As a matter of practice in many cases, we see judges and lawyers struggling to justify family law doctrine and decisions in terms of expectations arising from promises and consent, and so the contract concept is frequently on display implicitly in family law. But some attributes of marriage cannot be legally modified, and the model falls short for those. The search for the nuts and bolts of understanding between two parties to a marriage is often fruitless, because promises are abstract and general without discernable anticipation of the events ahead.

The Economic Model.   Building on the contractual model, many see marriage in fundamentally economic terms, as an institution that maximizes efficiency by permitting specialization of various sorts, from child rearing and market work to bill paying and social climbing. Specialization, sometimes called *role division*, lets two individuals achieve more than half of what they could on their own. Contract underlies this version of marriage, but the economic model tends to notice those aspects of promise that maximize wealth better than those that raise happiness or purposefulness. Proponents of this model usually seek to reward wealth-maximizing specialization while punishing waste and inefficiency.

Religious Model. As the history of marriage shows, for many people marriage can also be a religious covenant, either required by religious devotion or, if entered into, governed by religious expectations. People who view marriage as primarily religious will view its purposes, definitions, and expectations as pointing toward religious devotions. They frequently expect the law to either reflect those purposes directly or accommodate them indirectly. The law does incorporate religious understandings in some concrete ways, including granting religious authorities the right to officiate legally at a wedding and providing for annulments that have religious significance to some couples.

Partnership Theory. Other theories of marriage refine some of the ones above. Many scholars speak of the partnership theory of marriage, which posits that all work done by either party is done for the good of the partnership, and each contributes equally, even though they contribute differently. This is related to both the contract and the economic models of marriage, but unlike the economic model, particular behaviors receive less scrutiny, as the partnership is presumed to function for the common good. This model also invokes more traditional theories of marriage as a unity (all for one and one for all) because of its decreased emphasis on parsing out what each individual contributes.

Reproductive Model. Aligned with the religious model of marriage, some view marriage as reproductive at heart, with procreation, and possibly also child rearing, as its purposes. To those who see marriage this way, restricting entry into marriage based on the ability to procreate can make sense, and structuring family law for maximum stability and health for the rearing of children is thought to be the defining goal.

Companionate Marriage. Many people today believe that love, affection and companionship are the purpose and basis of marriage. People choose to marry each other based on that love and affection. As simple as it sounds, this concept of *companionate marriage* once reflected a radical departure from the duty-bound economic or religious institution of olden days. As we will show, the cultural acceptance of companionate marriage helps explain various modern characteristics of marriage, including the idea that exit from marriage may be appropriate when emotional satisfaction is absent, and the idea that marital contribution includes love and emotional support.

2. Roles in Family Law

Roles and role differentiation within couples are central to understanding family law. Many have criticized this attribute of family law. Roles denigrate individualism and diversity. Role analysis suggests expectations and stereotypes and narrows the ability to see the infinite range of behaviors couples negotiate and enact. Role *expectation* is indeed repressive.

But much of family law is built around the likelihood that adults within a marriage will differentiate, to some degree, from one another along a well-recognized set of behaviors. This is so as a matter of marital practice, whether a couple is ideologically opposed to role differentiation or comfortable with it. Those who endorse role neutrality must still contend with the fact that (1) it is not achieved in the overwhelming majority of marriages, (2) nor is it even a universally accepted aspiration, and (3) family law has deep roots in the practical consequences of that differentiation in a number of areas. The roles that have been most fully addressed in family law are provider, parent, consumer, saver, homemaker, caregiver, and dependent.

It is hard to explain much of family law if one removes discussion of roles from the analysis. Roles that family members have adopted serve as justifications for distributions of assets and income post-divorce and influence child-support and custody determinations. Roles within marriages also serve as justification for many institutional responses to couples during marriage, such as the extension of credit by financial institutions.

In recent decades, there have been significant changes in the role behavior of married couples up and down the income scale. Women have taken on a growing proportion of the financial provider role, as men have taken on a growing proportion of the caregiving and homemaking roles. These changes have complicated the analysis of roles in marriage, reduced the reliability of predictions and assumptions about behavior, and thus reduced the ability to do simple justice according to broad assumptions about facts. But the era of egalitarianism has not, as many had predicted or hoped, eliminated all ability to speak meaningfully about role differentiation, its determinants, and the appropriate responses to it. Rather, role differentiation has been destabilized but not eliminated. Study after study has confirmed that wives today do more homemaking and child-rearing work than their husbands, and husbands provide more financial support to their families, than vice versa.

The challenge to family role expectations in the last several decades has called into question many of the justifications for family law doctrines. At the same time, the newer expectations of role egalitarianism must contend with either the slow pace of real change or the very deeply entrenched nature of some of the differentiation that occurs within marriage. Many scholars of gender maintain that the home in general, and marriage in particular, is the primary forum for gender role performance. How family law should respond to the roles individuals do assume, without constraining or influencing the ability of individuals to craft their own marital expectations and participate in the evolution of marital expectations, is one of the great challenges for legal actors in this field. As we examine family law doctrines throughout this book, we will consider the way ideas about roles: archaic, modern, aspirational, empirical, and diverse, are operating.

3. Dependence

One does not have to think very long about the law of the family before one realizes that there is a chicken-and-egg problem at the root of the doctrine. Does family law exist to ensure that dependents' needs get met, or are dependencies created because of the way in which family law constructs roles and relationships? We will not offer chicken or egg as answer in this book, but we will talk about the ways both questions deserve affirmative responses. Family law does help ensure that dependents' needs get met, and it also helps create those dependencies. One's view of which came first may depend on whether one is inclined toward biological or social explanations. And, to the extent one likes to include elements of both the biological and the social in explaining contemporary phenomena, one is left without a definitive answer to which came first.

A biologist looking at the human condition, particularly the human condition as it compares with other animals, would likely note that the human female reproduces pursuant to a long and particularly onerous pregnancy process, during which it becomes harder for a woman to take care of herself. She is also primarily responsible for a particularly needy infant, who nurses and remains unable to care for itself for a long time. Unlike most children in the animal kingdom, human children remain unable to fend for themselves for many years after birth. The dependency of children begets the dependency of their caretakers because caretakers compromise their ability to take care of themselves when they care for others.[2] Thus, the biology of human reproduction may create dependencies in both women and children that necessitate social institutions charged with making sure that dependents' needs get met.

The constructs of marriage and parenthood serve as these social institutions.

At the same time, it is clear that the way in which our family law system constructs legal statuses can perpetuate dependency. For years, for instance, married women were not allowed to own property or make contracts for wages. Biology did not create a married woman's inability to provide for herself; the law did. Comparably, today, the ways in which the law refuses to honor much of the labor that women perform — physical and emotional caretaking, household organizational work — and refuses to afford married people the ability to contract with their spouses, undermines women's ability to provide for themselves. Biology cannot explain, for instance, why the law steadfastly refuses to treat family caretaking as labor worthy of remuneration. Indeed, a biologist might argue that women are undercompensated for their reproductive labor because the law often fails to acknowledge how much more resource intensive females' contribution to reproduction is. If, over the past several centuries, the law had been more vigilant in compensating women for their nonmarket labor, we might not view many women as dependent. We would view them as entitled.

4. Natural Families and Legal Creations

Throughout family law, we will see legal actors deciding whether to assign authority to what is viewed in a given case as biologically determined. While biological reproduction gives rise to some dependencies, many nurturing tasks are nudged in one direction by biology but are further cemented by social expectations and legal rules. Disentangling the influence of each on the allocation of nurturing roles has proved an elusive task.

This question of biological determinism has a discredited history in family law from when it has been used to govern mixed race families, sex-differentiated rights, child custody, and more recently same sex relationships. Courts struggle with the role that biology should play in understanding the parent-child relationship and continue to struggle with its role in same sex relationships. Many things once thought to have biological imperatives are now viewed as being legal or cultural creations, and doctrine has evolved as ideas about biology have advanced. Whenever a child is born, for instance, there is a biological family, including a genetic mother, a genetic father, and a child, but the extent to which the legal family needs to map onto the biological one is highly contested. Moreover, we now have the technological ability to manipulate and chart biology in ways that undermine many traditional legal assumptions about family relationships. The fact that same sex couples cannot yet reproduce using only their own genetic material makes some people think that they therefore should not be able to marry. We will see courts continue to struggle with the authority that should be given to biological arguments as they arise in new contexts.

5. Sources of Law

The law we discuss in this book is usually state statutory law, although there is some state common law, federal statutory law, constitutional law, and international law that has relevance also. The most traditional source of family law has been state common law doctrine, and in some areas common law doctrine continues to have limited areas of applicability. But for most topics, state statutory law has supplanted state common law. There have been several Uniform Marriage and Divorce Acts and several Uniform Parentage Acts, but the common law has never been the subject of a Restatement from the American Law Institute (ALI). In the late 1990s, a group was assigned to create the first Restatement. Instead, the ALI eventually published something called "Principles" of family law, instead of a Restatement. The Principles function more as another

Uniform Law or model statute would, attempting to craft an ideal formula, rather than a Restatement of the actual family law doctrine from the states. Explanations and notes incorporated into the ALI Principles are now sometimes used by litigators and courts in making arguments, but the Principles themselves have not been widely adopted in any state. In practice, the Principles may be cited most for the idea that seemed to motivate most of the drafters: Notwithstanding the discretion that has traditionally defined family law, it is important to apply predictable presumptions instead of vague standards in order to provide consistent results across like cases.

Longstanding federal practice and law limits federal court jurisdiction over family law matters. There is an explicit domestic relations exception to federal diversity jurisdiction, so federal courts never hear divorce cases, even though they routinely hear state law questions in other areas, including torts, property, and state statutory law. Nonetheless, the federal government has increasingly inserted itself into family law in the last several decades. Concerns over federally funded welfare programs led the federal government to mandate state child support guidelines, paternity procedures, and a range of other child-related laws, from abuse and neglect law procedures to adoption standards. In almost all cases, the federal government has required the passage of state statutes using its spending power. Occasionally the federal government has intervened more directly, as it did in 1996 with the passage of the Defense of Marriage Act, which defined marriage for federal law purposes and purported to allow states to ignore same sex marriages from sister states. Finally, a number of international conventions and treaties come into play in family law, addressing topics ranging from child kidnapping to the status of women in families.[3]

There is a U.S. constitutional law of the family as well. Over the years, the Supreme Court has had something to say about how the Constitution recognizes and protects family relationships. There is a clear tension between the state and constitutional rhetoric, though. Constitutional doctrine seems to suggest that individuals must have great freedom to form and practice their family relationships as they choose. State law often suggests something very different. For instance, the constitutional right to marry is grounded in liberty and privacy-based doctrine and suggests that the state cannot interfere with the symbolic, spiritual, and expressive functions that marriage serves for individuals. By contrast, the state law doctrine speaks more of marriage as a societal necessity, having its roots in the maintenance of a civil, stable social order. Contemporary constitutional interpretations talk of marriage as something with which the state should not interfere. States often adopt the earlier Supreme Court language and talk about marriage as a civil contract between a man, a woman, and the state.

There is also a notable discord when one compares the constitutional rhetoric of parenthood with the state law that adjudicates parental disputes. The constitutional rhetoric with regard to parenthood is at its most potent when granting great deference to parents (at least married parents raising their own legal children) to raise their children as they choose. Parents are entitled to this deference in part because raising children (like marrying) is thought to be central to one's expressive and self-constitutive rights and in part to preserve a place for civic education that is free of the state as protection against tyrannical indoctrination. The irony is that, at divorce or if parents were never married, the deference to child rearing that the state affords to married parents disappears. In the name of protecting children's best interests, state family law courts routinely make even the most mundane child-rearing decisions. By arbitrating decisions between two divorced or never-married parents, the state protects parental relationships by regulating precisely what it refuses to regulate — in the name of protecting parent-hood — when families are intact.

Courts assume responsibility for determining what is in a child's best interest because the state has what is known as a *parens patraie* interest in all children. The *parens patraie* doctrine vests the state with the power to protect all people under legal disability (usually children, very old people, and the mentally incompetent). Quite obviously, though, the *parens patriae* doctrine exists in considerable tension with the constitutional doctrine of parental rights.

Our task with this book is not to bring harmony to these discordant discourses but to highlight when and how the various sources of law interact with each other.

6. Family Diversity and Doctrinal Normativity

Historically, a fictional normative family has stood at the center of family law. That fictional normative family has changed over time. For example, the expected age of marriage has risen, the legal status of women within marriage has changed, the role of spouses in selecting a spouse has changed, the regard for children has changed, and the expectations of married women's relationship to paid labor has changed. The normative family has evolved, even as it has remained fictional. There has always been far more variation in family forms and practices, and diversity of family practices within diverse cultural traditions, than people generally suppose. The normative fictional family has been ideology, not demography. Marriage rates have never been as high as the normative family would suggest, many children have long had more than two parent figures in their household over the course of their childhood, and the model family during every period has unraveled when examined by demographers.

Nonetheless, a certain idealized image of a family influences doctrine during many periods, just as doctrine struggles to accommodate the reality of greater diversity in practices. Sometimes ideals of normativity are proclaimed at an abstract level by courts, while those courts deal practically with the problems of real families who do not fit the norm. But at other times, the ideals of normativity have led to harsh outcomes for many individuals whose practices differ from those held out as the ideal. As we proceed through the book, you will see a tension between legal actors trying to enforce a singular family norm and families presenting those legal actors with the many different practices that make up the universe of real families.

7. Two Family Laws

At times it appears that there are two family laws — one for people with resources and one for people without them. The wealthier one is, the more one has to worry about the law of marriage and the less one has to worry about the law of parenthood. The less money one has, the more the inverse is true. Middle-class and wealthy people care about the law of marriage because (1) they are much more likely to marry and (2) marriage may affect their wealth. The two may be related. Because getting married may give a spouse access to a partner's financial resources at divorce, marriage may be more important to those with resources. Low-income couples, who have little if any acquired property and minimal income streams to distribute, may care less about the financial incidents of marriage. Possibly for this reason, they are, and always have been, far less likely to enter state-licensed marriages.

State regulation of parenthood suggests an opposite dynamic. While all parents are concerned about the laws of parenthood at divorce or if they were never married because courts determine custody arrangements and child-support obligations, middle-class and wealthy parents are rarely at risk of losing their parental rights entirely. The parenting practices of a wealthy divorced parent will be thoroughly scrutinized by the state only if the other parent convinces a court to do so. The parenting practices of low-income adults, on the other hand, routinely come under state scrutiny. In part because they are less likely to marry, in part because they are more likely to receive state funding, and in part because they are more likely to need state services, the low-income people must worry much more about what the state thinks about how they parent. For instance, a wealthy parent with a substance abuse problem can acquire private health-care services for herself and private child care for her children, and the state will never know there is a problem. A low-income parent with a comparable problem must rely on the state for the provision of both her own health-care services and child-care services.

Once state actors involved in providing these kind of services become aware that there may be a parenting problem, the state begins a formal process of monitoring and evaluating parental behavior that often lasts the entirety of a child's life. The instability, financial need, and inability to provide constant care that result from poverty are often interpreted as signs of bad parenting, raising the question of whether a poor parent is, in the state's eyes, a good parent. The Supreme Court has also made clear that the privacy and autonomy interests served by letting most married couples parent as they choose can be subordinated to the state's interest in monitoring how its money is spent.[4] This means that low-income parents who receive any kind of state support for their children do not receive the deference to their parenting practices that wealthy or middle-class people do.

We will highlight these class distinctions when particularly salient, but our failure to highlight them does not mean they do no permeate most of the discussions in this book.

B. FAMILY CHRONOLOGY

Like many texts about family law, this book is organized as if family life had a chronology: a beginning, middle, and end. This structure treats family formation as a time of decision marking the beginning of family life, the middle or ongoing family life as a more stable period, and the end of family life as if it were defined by dissolution of a relationship between adults. In real families, though, there are regular new beginnings throughout the life cycle, as children are born or brought into families, parents leave and new adult relationships lead to new parent-child relationships, and dissolved spouses or partners in fact have ongoing relationships, either financial ones or through dual care and support of their joint children. Organizing by family chronology must be understood as a matter of convenience, rather than a map of the facts of family life.

ENDNOTES

1. *Maynard v. Hill*, 125 U.S. 190 (1888).
2. Scholar Martha Fineman is generally credited with this key insight about dependency begetting dependency. See Martha Albertson Fineman, THE NEUTERED MOTHER, THE SEXUAL FAMILY AND OTHER TWENTIETH CENTURY TRAGEDIES (1995).
3. See, e.g., the International Child Abduction Remedies Act (implementing the Hague Convention on the Civil Aspect of International Child Abduction), 42 U.S.C. Sec. 11601-11610 (2000); International Covenant on Civil and Political Rights, G.A. Res. 2200A(XX9) art 23. (1966).
4. *Wyman v. James*, 400 U.S. 309 (1971).

～ 2 ～

Family Formation

A. FAMILY FORMATION FOR ADULTS

Only one in four U.S. families consists of children living with both parents with those parents married to each other. Yet this model family is in many ways the baseline in much of family law. The legal system tends to assume this family, until the facts show otherwise, and tends to treat the needs of these families as the first order of priority.

People enter and exit families, as adults come together and as children arrive in households. This chapter looks at the law's role in family formation. We first look at the ways the law responds to the relationship between and among adults, before turning to the relationship between children and adults in the family-formation process.

As suggested above, marriage is the most complicated and most significant legal and cultural framework for classifying and understanding adult relationships. The process of entering a marriage, and the question of whether a couple may marry or is married, take on a different significance depending on what the legal consequences of marriage are during any given era. Thus, over time, the legal significance of marriage has changed dramatically. A few examples will show why entry into marriage can become a more or less important legal determination when the institution itself transforms legally. Through much of the nineteenth century, marriage radically altered women's legal identity, as they "merged" for legal purposes with their husbands and could no longer independently engage in such basic legal acts as entering into a contract or owning property. Until the middle of the twentieth century, if a child's parents were not married to each other the child was termed "illegitimate," and her rights as a child of her father in particular were diminished as a result. Deciding whether a marriage had been properly entered into, then, had greater consequences for children in that era than it does now, when marriage is less relevant to the legal understanding of the parent-child relationship. Similarly, sexual activity outside of marriage was subject to a risk of criminal prosecution until the middle of the twentieth century, and thus the existence of a marriage allowed for the only legally protected sex.

During the expansion of the welfare state in the twentieth century, marriage was used to determine eligibility for benefits such as Social Security or military widow's pensions, and whether a marriage was properly contracted influenced entitlement to government programs. By the mid-twentieth century, marriage was also used by private employers to determine eligibility for privately administered social welfare benefits, like health insurance and pension rights. This touches on one way legal marriage is used, which is to provide an easy administrative framework for determinations of dependency and need within families. A licensing process for marriage allows simple documentary proof of eligibility for large numbers of individuals that would not be possible in a more fact-driven inquiry into actual dependency among individuals.

We live in an era where many state and local governments confer recognition of various kinds on couples who are not legally married. For example, some states will take jurisdiction to divide the property of cohabiting couples who have separated in a way that they would not have before 1970. For those couples, proper entry into marriage is no longer the only path to government recognition of the relationship. In addition, many private entities, such as employers, common carriers, or hospitals, recognize non-marital relationships in the distribution of dependent benefits. A substantial body of the case law around the entry into marriage developed against a backdrop of significantly less protection for unmarried adult partners and their children than we have today.

Finally, over the course of the last half century, women's independent economic identities — from economic prospects to economic rights — have improved significantly, such that marriage is no longer the primary path to economic security for women. Without understanding the stark contrast between the legal status of married and unmarried women historically, it can be hard to understand why there is such a well-developed body of law on the question of whether a couple has successfully and legitimately entered a marriage relationship. Many law students today spend little time studying the formalities of marriage entry, sticking instead to the more substantive and timely questions of who may marry. But this history of real consequences explains the development of a body of law addressed to the validity of marriages under a range of peculiar circumstances.

We will cover the most significant legal consequences of marriage, both historical and current, through the rest of this book, but having a flavor of why it matters that a couple is married helps us to understand the significance of marriage entry. Despite the reduction in legal disabilities for unmarried adults and parents, and the increased entitlements available to unmarried couples, marriage remains the most rich and robust legal status a couple may create.

1. Getting Started: Ways to Enter a Legally Recognizable Relationship

We explain in this section the legal beginning of adult relationships. The legal beginning happens in one of four ways:

(1) licensed marriage, (2) other licensed institutions such as domestic partnerships, (3) common law marriage, and (4) other *de facto* statuses.

a. Formal Beginnings

The first two beginnings, licensed marriage and other licensed relationships, entail couples bringing law into their family lives deliberately, an act they likely view as the beginning of their legal connection.

Marriage. Couples apply for a marriage license from a state, and the license is generally signed by a person who is authorized by that state to officiate a marriage, such as a judge or a religious official. The license alone doesn't make a couple married. Generally, the marriage also requires a ceremony showing a present intent to marry in front of witnesses. Consistent with the requirements of intent and consent, a marriage may be annulled if it is obtained by "fraud." It is as much the ceremony that makes the legal marriage as the license — if there is a defect in the license (it has expired before the ceremony, for example), in most cases courts will strive to overlook the defect. But a failure to solemnize the marriage in front of witnesses with a moment of public agreement can be dangerous to a later finding that the marriage is valid. This speaks to one important feature of marriage — that it serves as a declaration of commitment to someone else in addition to the two spouses. This is consistent with the notion that marriage is not a wholly private matter between spouses but is designed to be "read" by third parties as well, to greater and lesser degrees historically.

After the ceremony, a copy of the license is ordinarily returned to the state, and the marriage is "official." When all of these things happen, we can determine both when the relationship acquired legal significance and what the parties believed they were doing. In each state, a statute provides the exact procedures for licensing and solemnizing a marriage, with differing provisions for details ranging from what the requirement of witnesses will be and who may officiate to what sort of blood tests must precede the ceremony.

Nonmarital Formalities. Similarly, in recent years a formal start for nonmarital relationships is often achieved through legal avenues. Many cities and towns, and several states, allow couples to register some form of *domestic partnership* or *civil union*. Like marriages, these are formally registered with some government office, whether at the local level in the case of most domestic partnerships or at the state level in the case of civil unions (though at least one state — California — has expanded its original limited grant of "domestic partnership" rights to include the kind of comprehensive rights conferral associated with civil union).[1]

In the case of *domestic partnerships*, the legal consequences of the registration are ordinarily enumerated, and they are limited by the limits on the authority of the government body that issues them: A city can only confer a change in the couple's status with respect to that city's laws. For example, the city can give the domestic partnership consequences with respect to its rent-control ordinance but not with respect to state-level income tax law. Private actors, however, may confer benefits such as health insurance based on a domestic partnership, and many do, using the registration as irrebuttable evidence of a commitment between the parties adequate to justify conferring private benefits. This is in an example of the government and nongovernment interplay of family law. In most cases, domestic partnerships are available to same sex couples only, because marriage is unavailable to them in the jurisdiction, but some cities make them available to any couple.

The states that have adopted *civil unions* use that term to refer to a more comprehensive status than most domestic partnerships. Where they exist, the authority to register a civil

union is conferred by state government. Unlike domestic partnerships, the legal consequences of a civil union are not enumerated. Instead, they are defined as encompassing whatever
legal consequences marriage confers under state law. Civil
unions have no influence under federal law and are rarely
recognized by sister states that do not themselves grant the
status. Because civil union grants all rights of marriage within
the state, it is a parallel institution to marriage for same sex
couples. This makes it both a more significant institution than
most domestic partnerships and also a more controversial one.
Civil union withholds only the label of marriage from same sex
couples, not the material benefits and burdens. It thus accents
the role that the government plays in controlling the social and
cultural meaning of the name "marriage." Perversely, this
nearly full grant of rights can seem particularly punitive
because it appears to retain a distinction for the sole purpose
of stigmatizing same sex couples by giving their unions, and
only their unions, a different name.

Over the course of decades, same sex couples have solemnized marriages in religious and secular ceremonies without
the benefit of approval from a government entity. In this
way, same sex couples participated in the debate over whether
marriage was a cultural or a legal institution, both claiming
marriage without licensure as cultural and protesting the
inability to obtain licenses for their relationships. Some
same sex couples who choose to enter a licensed civil union
use the term *marriage* to describe their ceremony, continuing
the tradition of contesting state control over the cultural and
religious aspects of the institution of marriage. Since the
advent of licensed marriage between people of the same sex
in Massachusetts, Connecticut, Iowa, Vermont, briefly in
California, and a number of foreign countries including neigh-
boring Canada, many committed same-sex couples have
chosen not to call themselves married unless the government
licenses the marriage. The precision used by same sex couples

in describing their status now serves as a way of protesting the majority of U.S. jurisdictions that will not license same sex marriage. The availability of same sex marriages in places has caused some couples to make a more public display of their marriage and commitment ceremonies in protest of marriage license denials.

b. Informal Beginnings

In much the way the beginning of an adult relationship may be recognized by governments through licensing of marriages or registration of domestic partnerships, a substantial body of case law has developed for deciding whether to recognize relationships begun without license or registration. Law students often resist the idea of bringing law into relationships if a couple has not chosen to do so deliberately through a marriage licensing scheme or civil union. The single moment of formalizing the relationship becomes consent for the countless ways government will intervene and attach consequences to that relationship. But this perspective probably overstates the legal consciousness most licensed couples bring to their decision making. There's no good evidence that marrying couples know even the most basic legal consequences of the decision to marry; the decision isn't motivated primarily by a desire for legal consequences, though it may be motivated by a desire to express commitment.

Often the law binds couples to the legal consequences of marriage if they have demonstrated marital-type commitment, regardless of whether they got a license. Thus, couples who have not formalized a relationship may nonetheless find themselves with the same legal questions that arise between married people: How should debts incurred for the benefit of both parties be paid off? How should jointly used property be distributed? How should the parentage of children born into the relationship be determined? Just like their married counterparts, many unmarried couples have not anticipated these issues nor developed views ex ante about how they'd like them resolved. Turning a blind eye to these questions by refusing jurisdiction over them is rarely a neutral act. It almost always penalizes the party whose contribution to the relationship is nonfinancial — the one who has played the female gender role — with money staying in the hands of the partner who brought it into the relationship. Over time, courts and legislatures have crafted post hoc remedies for couples who are together in some sense but have not formalized their relationship in a licensed marriage or civil union.

Common Law Marriage. Common law marriage, sometimes characterized as the original process of marrying, is still recognized in over a dozen states. Common law marriage does not require cohabitation for a set period of years, as many imagine. Formally, there are four elements of a common law marriage: capacity to marry (right age, not already married, e.g.), the present agreement to be married, cohabitation, and the couple holding itself out to the community as married. There is no ceremony needed; a couple holds themselves out by referring to each other as "my husband" or "my wife" to third parties or on documents. Most of today's typical cohabiting couples do not refer to one another as spouses or hold themselves out as married. They do not necessarily lead people to believe they are married because it is acceptable to be cohabiting without marriage. But there was a time when couples cohabiting did seek the cover of marriage and when it was reasonable to assume a couple living together were married, especially if backed up by evidence that they referred to each other that way. This prior social practice of referring to a cohabitant as husband or wife may be why people developed the misconception that living together for a period of years could lead them to be classified as common law spouses. But the law has never classified couples as married when they didn't hold themselves out as spouses, nor has it required any period of time to pass for those who do hold themselves out as married.

Even though common law marriage has been eliminated in three-quarters of the states, it can still reach into those states. A couple who has lived in a common law marriage state and met the criteria of a common law marriage while there will have their marriage recognized in all other states pursuant to the practice of giving full faith and credit to marriages that are legal in a sister state. So the reach of common law marriage is greater than the number of states that have chosen to preserve it — in theory at least. The practical reach to all 50 states is open to debate. States that have eliminated common law marriage bring their perspective to bear when their courts are asked to decide whether a marriage met the common law definition of another state. That skeptical eye puts couples in a different position than they would be litigating in a state that retains common law marriage. They will only receive recognition by a court in a state that eliminated common law marriage if their facts are airtight and permit no alternative conclusion.

A common law marriage is the equal of a licensed marriage for legal purposes. It can only be dissolved upon the death of one party or with a divorce. All the legal consequences of a licensed marriage attach to it. It is not a form of über-cohabitation; it is real marriage. But its inception tends to be examined retrospectively, in light of the facts under which a couple lived. An important distinction between relationships licensed at the outset and those that are not is that the latter may exist for a long period of time but may be legally recognized only at a point of dispute, such as a dissolution or death. At the point of legal inquiry, parties have a stake in proving or denying the marriage's existence that is usually at odds with the other's or with each other's heirs.

In different periods of history, common law marriage suffered no disrespect or lesser status than licensed marriage within some U.S. communities. Clergy were scarce or expensive, and it was conventional for couples to take up residence and refer to each other as husband and wife. Common law marriage was eliminated in a legislative movement at the beginning of the twentieth century for many reasons, including some high-profile cases in which fraud was alleged by a widower's parents, children or siblings who wished to deny a marriage had existed in order to collect the assets of the deceased, and with the rise in marriage dependent benefits and land claims that were easier to administer with clear documentation of a marriage. Those states that retain it today preserve a perspective on the marriage institution under which marriage is created by couples and communities, in the culture at large, and law simply recognizes a social fact that it did not create. The government takeover of licensed marriage that has occurred in the last century, by contrast, asserts a newly central role for the government in defining marriage itself, not simply its consequences.

Nonmarital Relationships Without Registration.

The last four decades have seen a significant increase in the number of unmarried but cohabiting couples. These couples are unmarried for a variety of reasons. The majority are cohabiting prior to marrying or cohabiting to see if marriage might be appropriate. They are not marriage dissenters, exactly, but consider cohabitation a step toward eventual marriage. Some cohabitants are not permitted to marry or register as domestic partners, as is the case for most same sex couples. But some cohabitants may view the decision not to marry as the best option for retaining control over the contours and expectations of their relationship. They may prefer to avoid the gender symbolism of marriage, the tax consequences, or the costly process of ending a marriage through divorce.

When cohabitation is significant in duration and individuals make decisions in reliance on the dependability of the relationship, courts have crafted a number of ways to intervene to settle a couple's financial entanglements or distribute a public benefit such as rent-controlled housing. Contract law is the main tool used for recognizing these relationships, although there are other tools as well. While judicial interventions are numerous, they are also fitful and unpredictable. Some courts, championing the state's role in defining and encouraging marriage, have refused to recognize any obligations between nonmarital cohabitants. To these courts, allowing people to secure some of the benefits of legal marriage without requiring them to formally enter it may undermine the state's role in defining marriage. Prior to the 1970s, most courts refused to enforce even an express contract between a cohabiting couple who were engaged in what was termed a *meretricious relationship*, meaning one that included sexual activity. If the cohabiting couple were committing the crime of fornication, any contractual agreements about property or income were understood by courts to be prostitution and were altogether unenforceable. This led to an absurd system where couples could actually execute written agreements about how their property should be divided in the case of a split and what financial support one might still provide to the other, and those agreements would not be enforceable if they were between cohabitants with a sexual relationship.

In 1976, the California Supreme Court decided the landmark case of *Marvin v. Marvin*,[2] which ushered in a sea of change in judicial understanding of cohabiting couples in California and in time nationwide. The *Marvin* court maintained that a couple could not bargain for sex itself, but it allowed that any express agreements between cohabitants would otherwise be enforceable. Further, the *Marvin* court expounded on the idea of an *implied contract* between cohabitants, whereby post-separation obligations might be judicially imposed based on the implicit promises the individuals made to each other through their conduct. The court invited a fact-based inquiry into the way the parties lived to see if there was a "tacit understanding" between the parties about property or support.

Conceptually, *Marvin*'s implied contract holding was a very significant development, as it opened the door to a finding of a legally consequential relationship based not just on explicit agreements, written or spoken, but on the agreement implicit in living in a marriage-like relationship and developing roles and dependencies in that relationship. The *Marvin* court reflected contract doctrine in the commercial setting, rejecting the idea that intimacy robs a court of the ability to evaluate implicit understandings arising from a course of conduct. That attribute of *Marvin* is honored most in the breach, with real cases of obligation based simply on "tacit" understanding being rare. Yet the idea appeared to echo common law marriage: Acting like a dependent couple could make you one for legal purposes.

While other states varied in the extent to which they absorbed *Marvin*'s doctrine of implied contract through tacit understanding, most have embraced its willingness to allow cohabiting couples to contract and will entertain the application of contract remedies such as constructive trust, *quantum meruit*, or partnership theory. They may not be as expansive in their judgments as *Marvin* claimed to be, but they do invite fact-based inquiry into the way a relationship is conducted.

The *Marvin* remedy leads to one of the great ironies of the request for legal recognition of the cohabiting relationship: It may be subject to a fact-finding about how a couple conducted their affairs that does not attend to the marriage relationship. Once licensed and solemnized properly, a married couple may choose to live unconventionally but generally will still receive the benefits of marriage laws and be understood to be legally married. Cohabitants, on the other hand, will be judged based on how conventionally they lived. Courts will investigate whether they shared a checking account, whether they were monogamous, and whether they actually provided each other with emotional support in deciding whether a relationship exists that warrants legal recognition. The validity of their relationship for legal purposes will depend on an inquiry that will invade the couple's privacy far more than the marriage decision would have. If a legally cognizable relationship is the goal, marriage, for those who can access it, may be the one that permits greater freedom to craft unconventional roles.

As long as the relationship is contractual, it can only influence the legal relationship between the parties, such as how they'll dispose of their property, but not the actions of third parties whom the couple cannot bind. Marriage, on the other hand, influences not only the relationship between the parties but also the way third parties respond to them, from the extension of credit to the filing of tax returns. For some limited third-party purposes, however, courts occasionally have been willing to find a legal relationship between cohabitants. One landmark case allowed a same sex partner survivor benefits under a New York rent-control law because he met the definition of *family* within the rent-control ordinance.[3] As in the case of cohabitation contracts, the finding of a relationship was a fact-driven inquiry into the conventionality of the relationship itself.

Thus, we see that cohabitants who do not wish to (or are not able to) marry or enter a civil union can enter a legally recognized relationship by signing a contract. If they do not enter into an express contract, the validity for legal purposes of the entry into their relationship will be a retrospective fact-based judgment. Therefore the entry into the relationship is marked with uncertainty for legal purposes: It may at some later date be judged to have given rise to legal obligations or consequences, but by accretion, without a single moment marking the entry into a legally consequential relationship. Couples wishing to retain independence from the risk of this sort of retroactive finding may do so with an express, written agreement disclaiming obligations, which would be decisive evidence of understanding and intent. But the need to take that step reflects an uncertainty in the default understanding.

Recognizing that unmarried cohabitants often need legal remedies for practical problems arising out of their relationship, some people have endeavored to craft solutions to the uncertain entrance into the relationship. The American Law Institute, for example, argues for marriage-like property consequences once a couple cohabits for two years. The Canadian family law code does something similar. But in U.S. jurisdictions, that kind of formal recognition of informal relationships has yet to fully bloom, and many scholars worry that imposing marital consequences on couples who have not married deprives some people of their ability to stay uncommitted. Because cohabitation has become so much more common, it can no longer be as readily used as an indication of commitment, thus the law may need to find new ways of finding genuine implicit commitment and dependency.

2. The Right to Marry

In 1967 the Supreme Court declared that there is a fundamental right to marry under the United States Constitution. That case, *Loving v. Virginia*,[4] struck down a Virginia criminal statute that punished a black woman and a white man for leaving the state to marry in a jurisdiction that permitted interracial marriage, returning to Virginia, and living as spouses there. The court ruled that the Virginia statute was both racially discriminatory under the equal protection clause and a violation of a fundamental right to marry, which the court located in the due process clause of the Fourteenth Amendment. This kind of *anti-miscegenation* statute was in effect in a majority of the United States in the first half of the twentieth century and existed in some places in some form dating back to the colonial era, with a brief reprieve during Reconstruction. But they had become increasingly controversial and had been struck down as early as 1948 in California under the Fourteenth Amendment to the U.S. Constitution.[5] During the 1950s, a number of states repealed their anti-miscegenation statutes, while Southern states maintained them.

Once the Supreme Court had declared a fundamental right to marry, courts had to struggle with whether all restrictions on the ability to marry must be necessary to serve a compelling state interest. Some restrictions have been put to that test and found wanting, including restrictions on welfare recipients[6] and prisoners.[7] Other restrictions, however, have not been subject to the fundamental rights analysis, because the restriction amounts to an incidental burden on marriage. The Court's language tells us that which test applies is a function of how serious the restriction is, but this often seems to be contradicted by the practice of courts. So, for example, restrictions on age, number of spouses, or incestuous marriages serve as absolute prohibitions on a marriage. To anyone wishing to contract such a marriage, it is not an incidental burden but a complete prohibition. Nonetheless, courts generally apply a rational basis test to these regulations, not the fundamental rights analysis apparently supported by *Loving* and used by some of the courts who have addressed the same sex marriage issue. The next section considers the specific restrictions on the entry into marriage.

a. Restrictions on Entry to Marriage

As long as states have issued marriage licenses, they have regulated who may marry and who may not. This authority has shaped the institution of marriage. Much of the time it has simply reflected cultural values, and some prohibitions continue to do so, such as the prohibition against sibling marriage or marriage of children. But at other times the state's gatekeeping role has navigated and shaped controversies over marriage. For example, some of the miscegenation statutes struck down in *Loving* had been adopted in an aggressive campaign to maintain racial segregation during the Jim Crow era, because similar laws had been repealed during the Reconstruction era. The states were using their authority to regulate marriage in a deliberate effort to engineer social behavior, and they criminalized rebellion against what the *Loving* court eventually acknowledged was a system of white supremacy. It was in the context of such deliberate social engineering and during a time when the country was in outright civil unrest over the injustice of the system of white supremacy that the Supreme Court found a fundamental right to marry as against such state intervention. We will first discuss the less controversial restrictions on entry to marriage and then elaborate on how the more controversial restrictions on marriage entry, particularly marriage between people of the same sex, reflect deep conflict about the extent to which the state is free to define what marriage is.

Age.   At common law the age of entry into marriage stayed close to puberty, with girls being prohibited from marriage under age 12, and boys under age 14. That age has risen and in most states rests between 16 and 18, with a lower age permitted in many states with the spouse's parents' permission. Some states allow a court to license a younger marriage under certain circumstances, most commonly in the case of a pregnancy. The age limits reflect our changing views of capacity to make significant decisions across many aspects of citizenship, including contracting, joining the military, voting, and driving.

Incest.   All states prohibit marriages between people of consanguineous relationships (blood), and many by affinity as well (such as a stepparent or uncle by marriage). These prohibitions have deep roots in many cultures, although the contours of them differ. For example, in some religious traditions a man is expected or even required to marry his brother's widow, while in others he is not permitted to. It is assumed that the incest prohibition is a piece of wisdom that presages genetics: Cultures absorbed the risk of birth defects that may be produced by the marriage of close relatives and regulated accordingly. This explanation for the historic ban as well as the contemporary one is probably weak. Genetic mutations that are shared by close relatives are likely to be expressed in their children. But those mutations are as likely to be positive as negative, and expression of negative mutations may be an important step in their elimination. Further, genetic counseling would be as sound an approach to this issue if it were the only thing complicating the match: The state would not prohibit the marriage of two unrelated people who carried genes guaranteeing the passage of debilitating illnesses to their offspring. Genetics offers a convenient, but likely inaccurate, explanation for the history of prohibiting incestuous marriage.

It seems more probable that incest is a universal prohibition because of the likelihood of disrupting family ties and responsibilities and injecting instability and sexual imposition into the necessary dependencies within families. The incest ban supports a norm of non-sexualized family space because it protects victims from the undue influence of older and more powerful family members. Each state takes its own approach to the degrees of consanguinity prohibited, and individual cases that could pose a challenge to this restriction are exceedingly rare. Here marriage law reflects cultural practices in an ordinarily uncomplicated and uncontroversial way.

Health Screening. While many states require health screening for communicable diseases before issuing a marriage license, some do not, and the information gleaned from these health screenings will not lead to the denial of the license.

Waiting Periods. Most states impose a waiting period between the time a couple applies for a license and the time they may marry. This period has been reduced to a period of a few days in most jurisdictions, and in a few there is no wait at all. The waiting period tracks the posting of banns in church history, which allowed for community objection based on information that might come to light during the waiting period, such as secret prior marriage or a character charge against one spouse. Today it appears to serve only as a check on a whimsical or impulsive marriage being solemnized moments after the decision to do so. This is said to occur in Las Vegas, where there is no waiting period.

Void Versus Voidable Marriage. A marriage that has been solemnized but is later found to have a defect may be termed either *void* or *voidable*, depending on the circumstances and the defect. For example, an incestuous marriage will always be void, meaning it cannot be repaired and is permanently and immediately invalid *ab initio*, meaning from the outset. However, some marriage defects will lead to a determination that the marriage is voidable by one party if they choose to end it, but not void automatically. An example would be an age restriction where all parties accept the facts of the age restriction but wish to remain married, because the parties will grow to be the appropriate age. Another example would be one party's fraudulent representation as to some material fact of the marriage, such as known inability to engage in sexual relations. In that case, the marriage is only voidable historically, meaning the "aggrieved" party may choose to validate or void the marriage but is not required to. The notion of a voidable marriage had far more salience when divorce was largely unavailable without real cause, and the determination that a defect made a marriage voidable created an "out" for one party to the marriage.

Plural Marriage. In the era before divorce was available, marriages often ended with abandonment. Given the poor state of long-distance communications, a person could walk away from his marriage in Maryland and set out for the prairie states to begin again. He might enter into a new common law marriage in Kansas. Because divorce was generally not available, he could be prosecuted for bigamy if he were found out, and so could his first wife in Maryland if she remarried. Such was the early state of bigamy prosecutions — a woman remarried years after her spouse left town on what was supposed to be a short journey, assuming that he had died, only to find later he was still alive, and she now a bigamist. Exceptions were made for those who were missing on the high seas for a long period of time, but otherwise, no mistakes were allowed as defenses to such prosecutions: Bigamy was a strict liability crime.

Polygamy is a different practice than the fraudulent bigamy described above. Polygamy is practiced openly among the spouses, with all parties knowing about multiple parties to the marriage. The Model Penal Code punishes polygamy practiced with a claim of a right more harshly than polygamy practiced by fraud. In other words, at least the Model Penal Code considers it more threatening to have polygamists claim legitimacy than to have bigamists causing individual damage to individual parties unaware that they are sharing a spouse. In this regard, law again intervenes to define and legitimize some marriages and delegitimize others — law is active in shaping norms. Polygamy, after all, has historically been the world's most common form of marriage. It is described without criticism in the Hebrew and Christian bibles and has been practiced across the globe. There are surely reasons to disapprove of the practice, but our point is that the legal system in the United States makes illegal and illegitimate a social and cultural practice with extraordinarily deep roots. The law is not simply acting as an impartial administrator of cultural family practices. It is choosing among them in much the way it does with same sex marriage and interracial marriage.

During the era of the founding of the Church of the Latter Day Saints (Mormons), whose early followers believed that polygamy was required by God, states aggressively prosecuted polygamous marriages contracted by members of that faith. During the nineteenth century, Mormons unsuccessfully challenged those prosecutions as violations of their religious liberty. Without a great deal of elaboration, courts declared that monogamy reflected core cultural values and polygamy did not. Therefore polygamy could be criminalized, as bigamy always had been. Eventually, Mormons rejected and abandoned the practice of polygamy. Its permanent and unamendable prohibition was written into the Constitution of the state of Utah in the bargaining process that allowed Utah to join the union. Polygamy is still practiced by tens of thousands of Fundamentalist Latter Day Saints (FLDS), and more recent attempts to claim a religious liberty against prosecution for polygamy have been rejected as well. In fact, polygamy has been successfully prosecuted even when the perpetrator made no claim to be legally married to more than one person at all but only to be religiously married. In 2001, the state of Utah found a common law marriage to the defendant's first wife and then cohabitation with the subsequent wives sufficient to constitute the crime of polygamy, although the defendant was purporting to engage in private conduct outside of the sphere of legally licensed marriage.[8]

Opposite Sex Requirement. At this writing, only the states of Massachusetts, Connecticut, Iowa, and Vermont license marriage between people of the same sex. California did so briefly in 2008 between a court decision requiring issuance of licenses to couples of the same sex and a ballot referendum amending the state constitution to prohibit them. Most state statutes setting out the conditions for obtaining a marriage license did not mention the requirement of one man and one woman until very recently, in direct response to the movement to license marriage between couples of the same sex. The opposite sex requirement was assumed and not challenged until the 1970s, and those early cases dismissed the idea of a license for couples of the same sex out of hand, in much the same way that courts had dismissed polygamy.

It was not until 1993 that the Supreme Court of Hawaii became the first high court to find that the prohibition on marriage between people of the same sex was subject to the state constitution's equal protection provision because it discriminated on the basis of sex.[9] During the subsequent trial on whether the state could meet its heavy strict scrutiny burden in defense of the law, voters in Hawaii amended their constitution to allow the state legislature to define marriage as between a man and a woman. The legislature did so but simultaneously created a "reciprocal beneficiaries" status that could be used by same sex couples to obtain many of marriage's benefits — the first such status at a state level in the country.

That process in Hawaii became a harbinger of things to come in other states. In 1999, the Vermont Supreme Court found that same sex couples were entitled to all the rights and obligations of marriage.[10] The court decided the case under the Vermont Common Benefits Clause, which loosely parallels an equal protection clause. The Vermont Supreme Court did not find that same sex couples were entitled to the status of marriage itself, only all its legal incidents. The court allowed the legislature to choose whether to create a new status or give same sex couples entry into marriage. The legislators of that state responded in 2000 by choosing to create the first "civil union" status that gave same sex couples all the benefits of marriage conferred by that state's laws while denying those couples the marriage status itself. After nine years of issuing licenses for civil unions, in 2009 Vermont became the first state to approve same sex marriages through the legislative process instead of the courts.

In 2003, the Massachusetts Supreme Judicial Court decided *Goodridge v. Department of Public Health*, which struck down the state's opposite sex marriage requirement, and in 2004 Massachusetts became the first state to issue marriage licenses to couples of the same sex.[11] The court in *Goodridge* found that there was no rational basis for denying marriage to same sex couples, particularly in light of prior state policy supporting parenting and adoption by same sex couples and prohibiting discrimination against same sex couples in other contexts. It thus avoided any question of whether there is a fundamental right to marry under either an equal protection or due process analysis. At the same time, the opinion in *Goodridge* recognized that the importance of marriage did not rest only in its legal benefits and burdens, but as much in its cultural and social significance.

From 2004 to 2008, Massachusetts stood alone in granting marriage licenses to same sex couples. But cases challenging the state law prohibitions against same sex marriage wound their way through the courts of a number of states during this period, and legislators took notice. This litigation, often taking several years within each court system, prompted deliberation in state legislatures over whether and what rights should be granted by statute to same sex couples. Many legislators were moved by the pleas for equal treatment of and on behalf of their gay and lesbian consistuents. Some pragmatic legislators weighed the likelihood of impending court-ordered action of some sort and were prompted to act ahead of an order to do so. Some hoped action in the legislature to provide enumerated benefits, or even civil unions, might lessen the likelihood that the court would decide that the rights of state citizens were being violated by the denial of marriage. Others sought to create legislation in advance of a court order to be on the right side of history, avoiding the embarrassment of providing civil rights only when ordered to, not independently. Still others, such as the California legislature, followed Hawaii in passing legislation that would counteract ballot initiatives that had damaged hope of equality for same sex couples in the state.[12] During those years, several state legislatures, including Connecticut, New Jersey, and California, followed Vermont's lead and instituted civil union status statutes for same sex couples. But only New Hampshire passed a civil union statute without pending litigation in the state on the status of same sex couples. The New Jersey legislature acted after a New Jersey Supreme Court opinion finding similar to that of the Vermont court: that gays and lesbians had an equality right to all of the legal incidents of marriage, although they did not have a fundamental right to marriage itself.[13] Several other jurisdictions, including Maine, Oregon, Washington, and the District of Columbia, instituted lesser domestic partnerships, giving some measure of benefits to same sex couples but not intended to confer legal benefits equivalent to marriage.

In 2008, two high courts in states that already provided all of the incidents of marriage to same sex couples ruled that maintaining two different kinds of marital regimes, marriage for opposite sex couples and civil unions for same sex couples, violated that state equal protection clauses. The California Supreme Court so ruled in May of 2008.[14] The Connecticut Supreme Court followed suit in October of 2008.[15] Then, in November 2008, voters of California passed Proposition 8, a ballot initiative that changed the state constitution to define marriage as between a man and a woman.

In 2009, the Iowa Supreme Court held that state law prohibiting same sex marriage violates its state equal protection guarantee. The following week, the Vermont legislature voted to license same sex marriage. This vote was a milestone for same sex marriage, marking the first time a legislature affirmed the right. At the time of this writing, Massachusetts, Connecticut, Iowa, and Vermont are the only states that recognize full marriage rights for same sex couples.

Courts and scholars locate the right to same sex marriage in one or both of two constitutional doctrines common to state constitutions as well as the U.S. Constitution: fundamental right to marry or equal protection of the law. The Supreme Court found a fundamental right to marry in *Loving v. Virginia*. But critics of the fundamental right theory argue that the claim does not yield a definitive answer because a fundamental right to marry presupposes a definition of marriage. It is precisely that definition of marriage that is contested: Is marriage inherently heterosexual or not?

More of the courts that have voted in favor of same sex marriage have used an equality theory, which the *Loving* court also relied on. Within the equality line of jurisprudence, there are questions of whether the equality right is best conceived of as a right to be free from gender discrimination or a right to be free from sexual orientation discrimination. Gender discrimination is more widely acknowledged to be a right protected in constitutional law. But many people do not recognize a prohibition on same sex marriage as a problem of sex discrimination, because both men and women are prohibited from changing the definition of marriage from an opposite sex union to a same sex union. Protection from discrimination on the basis of sexual orientation might be a more promising approach, because denying gay and lesbian people marriage strikes at the core of their identities by regulating their family affiliations. But sexual orientation is not recognized by most states as a protected class under their constitutions, nor is it recognized as such under the United States Constitution. If sexual orientation is not defined as a suspect classification, no heightened scrutiny is paid to disparate treatment on that basis.

In response to events of recent years, some ask whether the state should license marriages at all or instead leave that task to religious and cultural institutions while licensing only civil unions for legal purposes. The source of the right to marry may have implications for whether the state must license marriage at all. Ordinarily, rights are conceived as requiring noninterference by the state in private action, rather than affirmative enabling by the state — as wobbly as that distinction is in practice. Does placing a right to marry under the substantive due process clause, as the court did in *Loving*, suggest that the state must somehow enable marriage or provide people with the opportunity to marry? In the *Loving* case itself, the state of Virginia had not just failed to enable an interracial marriage with a license; it had criminally punished a marriage lawfully licensed in a different state. The court struck down the state's criminal prohibition, suggesting a noninterference perspective. But in declaring a fundamental right to marry, the definitional issue may have returned. If marriage was understood by the court to be defined by a state-issued license, then the court implicitly suggested that states must enable marriage affirmatively through a licensing scheme. It depends on what the nature of marriage is to which we have a fundamental right: a state-licensed institution or a pre-legal declaration of union. The state-licensed version of marriage that the fundamental right seems to embrace in *Loving* sits uncomfortably against a history of marriage as a religiously regulated institution recognized as common law with or without a license.

Alternatively, placing a right to marry under the fundamental rights prong of the equal protection clause, as the Supreme Court did in *Zablocki v. Redhail* and *Turner v. Safely*, suggests that the state could deny people the right to marry as long as it did not discriminate in that denial. The state could get out of the marriage business altogether — in doing so it would not be providing marriage to some and not others. By analogy, Prince Edward County, Virginia, responded to the requirement that states must provide equal access to integrated public schooling by closing down public schools entirely; there is no right to public schooling under the United States Constitution, only a right to receive public benefits equally. If equal protection is the basis for a possible right to same sex marriage, and objection is fueled in part by private religious tenets, states could avoid the controversy by eliminating state licensed marriage in favor of civil unions for all citizens, as numerous people have suggested. If the name *marriage* derives its importance from its cultural and symbolic meaning, perhaps the government has no place licensing the name at all. The state could instead allocate the legal incidents of marriage through civil union status to both same sex and opposite sex couples and leave it to religious or other cultural institutions to confer whatever it is that the name marriage represents.

When same sex marriage is adopted legislatively, as it was in Vermont, no constitutional argument is necessary.

The rich debate over how to expand legal recognition of same sex relationships may obscure the reality that since *Baehr v. Lewin* was decided in 1993, many more states have moved to limit the rights of same sex couples than to expand them. As of this writing, 43 states now have statutes or constitutional amendments that define marriage as between a man and a woman. Some go further, limiting the ability of state legislatures to create civil unions or domestic partnership laws. Many of those states also have laws prohibiting the recognition of a gay marriage or civil union formed in another state.

Congress passed the federal Defense of Marriage Act (DOMA) in 1996.[16] DOMA allows the federal government to ignore any state law recognizing marriage between people of the same sex and encourages states to ignore any other state's same sex marriages. The federal DOMA and all the state-level "mini-DOMAs" have created a chaotic situation in the courts, as state after state must litigate whether a mini-DOMA prohibits a state university from giving partnership benefits to its employees, or how far the state may go in denying full faith and credit to judicial findings from a sister state pertaining to a same sex relationship. As there was with interracial couples during the time leading up to and following *Loving v. Virginia*, there is significant cultural conflict over the status of same sex couples, and the governments of the states are not simply reflecting uncontroversial practices but are deliberately shaping the marriage institution in one direction or the other.

The status of marriage between people of the same sex is in flux. Following the 2008 ballot initiative in California repealing same sex marriage, the movement for marriage held numerous of its highest profile protests yet throughout the country. Wthin six months, the movement for marriage had enormous victories in Iowa, which was the first unanimous opinion in favor of same sex marriage, and in Vermont, which became the first state to approve same sex marriage in the legislature. In the five short years after Massachusetts licensed the first same sex marriages in the United States, public opinion has become remarkably more favorable. Polling suggests a generation gap on the issue, with a majority of younger Americans supporting the rights of gay men and lesbians to marry, and the level of support declining with age. Many predict that we will soon reach a tipping point in support among the electorate due to this demographic feature of the controversy, at which point marriage rights will extend more broadly. But we are not there now, and translating increasing public support into legal change against an organized opposition whose views are strongly held is not a straightforward task.

3. Pre- and Postmarital Agreements

Family law scholars debate whether and in what ways marriage may be described as a contract between the parties or a status conferred by law and culture. While the notion that a marriage is a contract may have intuitive appeal, the marriage obligates and influences far too many third parties, and the rules applied to it may be modified too easily by the state without the parties' consent, to be a contract between the spouses. Contract works in part as a metaphor when describing contemporary marriage: Spouses choose one another for their own reasons, not for familial or community ones. People expect marriage to advantage both individuals, and satisfying these individuals is now the core of the arrangement. But beyond metaphor, contract also plays a legal role in marriage, albeit a more limited role than the nonlawyer might guess.

Some aspects of marriage may be viewed as contractual in that a written agreement between the spouses may modify the legal consequences of the marriage. Increasingly in recent decades, courts will look favorably on enforcing contracts signed in anticipation of marriage, or "prenuptial contracts," that modify some of the legal consequences of marriage.

Prenuptial agreements are interesting but still rarely executed. Their original use is still their most common one: to protect the inheritance of one spouse's children by a first marriage from a claim by a second spouse for an elective share of the estate. An elective share is a share that goes to a person's spouse upon his or her death. It is generally one-third of an estate, and the share overcomes any statement in a properly executed will to the contrary. In other words, if a 60-year-old woman decides to remarry after the death her first husband, she cannot simply write a will that will leave all her property to her children, bypassing her new husband. She needs to execute a prenuptial agreement to that effect.

Prenuptial agreements executed by couples who embarking on what may not be a long-term marriage are a better test of the extent to which marrying parties may "contract" around the basic terms of a legal marriage. Over time, the treatment of all prenuptial agreements has changed. At one time they would only be enforced if they addressed property distribution at the time of a spouse's death (the most common agreement), but no other terms would be enforced.

During the 1970s and 1980s, courts began to enforce prenuptial agreements at the time of divorce as well. But they did not enforce them under ordinary contract conditions. Instead, courts required a very high degree of procedural protection at the time an agreement was executed, which might include the requirement of counsel, an understanding of the other person's assets, an understanding of the legal rights being waived, adequate time before the wedding to consider the terms, and so forth. All these procedural conditions would be considered when deciding whether to enforce the agreement at the time of divorce. The idea behind procedural fairness may be that the couples are fiduciaries, not arm's-length negotiators, and have a greater responsibility for each other's welfare. In addition, it may reflect courts' appreciation of the cognitive biases — optimism in particular — and emotional strain surrounding marriage entry. Similar biases may attend the entry into other contracts that nonetheless lack special procedural protections. Courts either see the strains better in this context, or substantive views about prenuptial agreements and the nature of marriage are masked in procedure.

In addition to the procedural protection, many courts evaluated the fairness of the substantive terms of the agreement. An agreement that provided something for the "losing" spouse would be more likely to succeed than one that provided nothing. Moreover, the substantive fairness would be evaluated both as it appeared at the time the agreement was signed and as it appeared in light of the facts of the marriage. In other words, if the marriage were long and the financial dependence great and justified, the substance of a premarital agreement that left the dependent spouse with little would seem less fair when the divorce arrived than it did at the time it was signed. A court might refuse to enforce the agreement if the years had made it less substantively fair. This kind of *ex post facto* analysis departs from ordinary contract doctrine. It reflects a perspective about marriage as a state-conferred status, the obligations for which come as a package deal, not a menu. The trend has been away from strict substantive evaluation before enforcement, though some states still purport to require it. The heightened procedural fairness is still required in most jurisdictions. On either measure, the law of premarital agreements does not conform to ordinary contract law. It is subject to greater judicial oversight and thus less certain enforcement. If aspects of marriage are contractual, it is not entirely a contractual institution, and the state remains an important source of authority for the meaning and content of a marriage.

Practically, today, most premarital agreements entered into by younger couples involve considerable amounts of money, and the receiving spouse's financial entitlements under the contract, even if less than what the law might otherwise give, are still substantial. If the recipient spouse's award in the contract is large, courts are more likely to enforce the agreement. This means that wealthy individuals can still gain some predictability if they are willing to execute a reasonably generous agreement.

As a further sign of the limited ability to contract around the state's understanding at the outset of marriage, the terms that will be enforced in a premarital agreement are also very limited. Divisions of property are the most likely provisions to be accepted, and financial support payments only somewhat less likely. But contracts over anything else are extremely unlikely to be accepted. Perhaps because of the state's *parens patraie* authority and its attendant duty to take care of children, courts will not enforce any contractual provisions with regard to children (how many to have or how they are to be raised or how they will be provided for, for instance). Courts will not enforce contractual provisions pertaining to behavior during the marriage. These might include agreements about how often the couple will have sex, who will do which chores, how much weight one party to the agreement may gain, or whether in-laws will be permitted to visit or reside with the couple.

All of these nonmonetary attributes of a relationship may be written in an agreement and serve some therapeutic role for the parties. But courts have largely refused to enforce these terms, arguing that these are "essential" to a marriage and so nonmodifiable. By implication, the monetary terms might be viewed as less essential by courts, since courts will enforce the efforts of individuals to modify the background rules. But modifications to the essential terms are never enforced.

The state takes no independent position during a marriage on who will do what chores, how often a couple will have sex, or how much weight the parties gain. All it can do is rest financial consequences at divorce and death on its own criteria, either taking into account the parties' adjustments at the outset (when those deal with finances) or choosing not to (when they address more unusual topics). Still, the enforceability limits shed some light on what two people are doing when they enter marriage: They are stepping into a realm with legal consequences that will not be of their own choosing, will not be predictable and may change over time, and are likely not contemplated or understood by them.

Many states now also enforce postnuptial agreements. These are contracts signed by the parties while married. Most often, postnuptial agreements amend prenuptial agreements, but sometimes couples who have no prenuptial agreement enter into a postnuptial agreement. Like prenuptial agreements, postnuptial contracts are usually enforced only to the extent that they allocate property and income, and, like prenuptial contracts, they are usually only used by couples with extensive resources. While premarital agreements have the marriage itself as consideration, courts have struggled to find consideration for postnuptial agreements. Some courts have viewed continuation of the marriage, instead of divorce, as consideration, while others have been less comfortable viewing the threat of divorce as equivalent to the threat of breaking a plan to marry. A postnuptial agreement can be particularly troubling where one party asks for an advantage in exchange for staying in the marriage, the other party agrees to give up rights in that exchange to save the marriage, and subsequently the first spouse exits the marriage anyway with newly advantageous terms. Courts are aware of these risks and have used the consideration doctrine to scrutinize the conduct of parties seeking enforcement of a postnuptial agreement.

Marrying or married couples who have reason and inclination to sign legal agreements adjusting or clarifying the legal consequences of their marriage are uncommon. They are also likely atypical in their greater attention to legal obligations and risks associated with the marriage decision. Courts have moved toward treating their choices as largely practical and away from treating them as a symbolic threat to the meaning of marriage. Surely this is influenced by the changes in family characteristics of the late twentieth century: individualism, acceptable and common divorce, and women's increasing economic power. But enforcement of agreements is likely made easier by the atypical nature of couples who enter them, because courts may imagine that greater legal sophistication correlates with more deliberate choices.

B. FAMILY FORMATION: THE MAKING OF A PARENT-CHILD RELATIONSHIP

Just as the law recognizes and responds to the formation of adult relationships, adults and children become connected to each other and gain legal recognition for their connections. The mechanisms for establishing adult-child legal bonds are a product of many social forces. Children's dependency and need for adults is urgent. Adults in turn develop intense emotional attachments to children in their care. The human reproductive process leaves biological paternity uncertain.

But technology can now reduce that ambiguity and thereby gives rise to new tensions between biology and emotional attachments. Law attempts to respond and adjust to an increasing array of potential connections between adults and children in the service of deciding who will have legal rights to a child's company and who will be responsible for a child's dependency.

There are a number of official ways for an adult and child to establish a legal familial relationship. Parent-child relationships can be created by some combination of genetic link and statute, by marriage, by legal declaration (paternity and adoption), and sometimes, in cases involving noncoital conception, by contract. Like marriage, however, whether the parties actually act like parents has a good deal to do with whether a court will eventually treat them as parents. This chapter will explore all of these paths to parenthood.

1. Genetic Connection and Legal Parenthood

For every child born there is a man who provided sperm, a woman who provided an ovum, and a woman who gestated the fertilized egg. For most of human history, the law could assume that the ovum provider and the gestator were one in the same woman, and the law recognized that woman as the mother. Less accurately, the law assumed that the mother (if married) was married to the man who had fertilized the egg, so it called her husband the father. Thus, the norm upon which the law of parentage has always been based is one of a married couple giving birth to their own genetic issue. For years, that norm was rigidly enforced.

In the Anglo-American tradition, there was an irrefutable presumption that the husband of a mother was the father of a child. In medieval England, for some time, neither husband nor wife could testify to what was euphemistically referred to as "non-access." In other words, the law declared parenthood in the husband of the mother, regardless of whether either he or his wife knew facts that would make genetic fatherhood unlikely or impossible.[17] The irrefutability of the marital presumption dissipated some over time, but the practical problems of proving paternity prior to genetic testing helped keep the marital presumption extraordinarily strong. Thus, it has been marriage, more than genetics, that has determined fatherhood for children born into a marital family. The influence of that history is still visible in many aspects of parentage law, despite tremendous changes in the field. Genetic testing has made biological paternity more relevant to legal paternity, but it has not become controlling as some might guess.

Today, the marital presumption, and all presumptions of parenthood, are found in state parentage acts. Many people may think of parenthood as a natural or prelegal fact. But it is state statutory law that vests parental status for legal purposes. Most parentage acts simply state that the woman who gives birth to the child is the mother, although some states now have statutory provisions that allow surrogacy contracts to trump a presumption of motherhood in the woman giving birth.

Fatherhood is more complicated. Virtually all parentage acts retain a marital presumption, granting paternal status to the husband of the mother. But men in other situations are also presumed to be fathers. A man who signs the birth certificate, and a man who lives with the child for a given period of time after birth and holds himself out as the father, and a man who voluntary signs an acknowledgment of paternity are all presumed to be fathers ordinarily. The legal paternity of a child born to an unmarried woman is often a function of one of these other presumptions.

In a change from the past, all of these presumptions can be challenged today, usually by the mother, a presumed father, or by any man claiming to be the genetic father. But states have different standing and statute of limitations rules that make these challenges more and less meaningful. Because states are worried about the effects of leaving a child without any father, parentage statutes often limit the time within which someone who is presumed to be a father can challenge the presumption. But they do not necessarily limit the time within which someone can bring a claim to establish a parental relationship. In other words, it is easier to get into fatherhood than get out of it.

Under the U.S Constitution at least, marriage dominates genetics in determining who a parent is. The U.S. Supreme Court has upheld a state's ability to deny standing to an outsider to the marriage. The Court continues to respect the tradition of using marriage to convert a husband into a father. In upholding from constitutional challenge a law that let a man's marriage to a mother trump another man's biological paternity in deciding legal paternity, Justice Scalia declared that "California law, like nature itself, makes no provision for dual paternity."[18] Invoking nature, which we presume means biology or genetics, for the proposition that a child cannot have two fathers, Justice Scalia ironically upholds the dominance of the marital father over the genetic father, who was an interloper to the marriage. Today the California statute at issue has been modified to permit standing to an outsider. But the court's ruling illustrates the dynamic between biology and legal parenthood even in this era of more reliable information about biological links.

Law has slowly responded to the availability of new technology, though without making genetics decisive. Most parentage acts now seem on the surface to suggest that the relevant evidence for establishing or disestablishing a paternal relationship will be genetic. Indeed, if none of the presumptions of paternity apply, then a child or his mother usually must rely on DNA evidence to prove paternity. This marks a tremendous shift from the law of 30 years ago, when blood tests, if they were even available, were incapable of determining genetic connection with certainty. Without reliable genetic testing, plaintiffs in paternity actions used to have to bring claims based on the alleged facts of conception. Hence, paternity proceedings were about alleged sexual encounters. Now, they are mostly about DNA.

Despite what the wording of the statutes would seem to suggest, however, DNA does not always trump in a litigated paternity action. Judges have assumed that in cases of contested paternity, the best interest of the child should be considered. For instance, sometimes in a contested case, judges award parental status to a non-genetically related man who has acted as a father, does not want to relinquish paternal status, and has done what the judge perceives as a decent job of parenting. Other times, judges are faced with a non-genetically related man who *does* want to relinquish parental status but who cannot locate the genetic father. In these cases, judges often refuse to "release" a non-genetically related man from parental status (and the child support obligations that accompany it). Comparably, judges who are faced with a man who failed to question his genetic connection when he first learned that there might be reasons to be suspicious can avoid the biology question with notions of laches or reliance. In other words, biology does not decide fatherhood in contested cases. Often it is just one factor in determining paternal status. Sometimes it is not even that, as when judges augment presumptions with a best interest of the child standard to determine parenthood and disregard blood tests or refuse to order them in the first place. To a certain extent, this judicial maneuvering reflects a desire to make sure a child has two solid sources of financial support. But it also reflects the law's allegiance to a two-parent normative family. Courts are reluctant to leave a child with only one parent or to grant a child three.

Today, the vast majority of paternity actions involve neither competing presumptions of fatherhood nor tabloid-worthy allegations of casual sex with a rich and famous potential father.

They involve the government suing men who have been named as potential fathers by recipients of public assistance. In part because low-income couples are less likely to marry, and in part because government subsidies for low-income families are different than government subsidies for middle-class and wealthy families, parenthood is frequently determined differently depending on class. The federal government requires mothers applying for public assistance to name a father from whom the state can attempt to recoup assistance funds. By contrast, a middle-class mother is not asked to name the father of her child before she can receive a mortgage payment deduction on her income taxes if she owns her own home. Many of the mothers forced to name a father do not particularly want to establish paternity in the child's biological father. They recognize that the father does not have many, if any, resources to share, and they know vesting parental status in someone else will restrict their own freedom as parents. If a relationship with the biological father was violent or emotionally abusive or fraught with other difficulty, and the biological father is likely unable to pay, there is little the mother has to gain from naming him as a father.

Once the state has the name of a putative father, the state will institute a paternity suit. If successful, the state may garnish the wages or otherwise secure monetary contributions from the genetic father. The state keeps any funds collected from the father, up to the amount that it has paid out in assistance for his child, with the exception of $50 each month. The $50 is given to the mother as an incentive for her to name the father and cooperate in the paternity and child support action. Because they are subject to genetic testing, the men named in these suits may be secure in the knowledge that they are genetically related to the children for whom they are legally responsible. For most fathers who do not take a DNA test, meaning most middle- and upper-class fathers, paternity is a matter of trust and statute.

2. Adoption

Not all people become parents by biologically conceiving — or thinking that they have biologically conceived — a child. Some people adopt. Adoption involves two critical regulatory steps. The existing parent(s) must relinquish parental rights, and the adoptive parent(s) must accept them. Traditionally, it was only the mother who had to relinquish parental rights in most cases, and single parents were not eligible to adopt. Today, both of those practices have changed. Both mother and father must relinquish parental rights, and many states allow single parents to adopt.

The first adoption statute was passed in this country in 1851. It is probably fair to say that the concern of the legislature then was in securing "good" homes for children. Some children were genuinely in need of new homes due to death or illness of parents. Others were moved against the will of their parents. Perhaps not surprisingly, what counted as a "bad" home for children was a function of class and ethnic bias. Many immigrants in this country were cajoled into giving up their children so that their children could have a better life than the one they were likely to inherit in the poor urban neighborhoods of their parents. The adoption of immigrant children fit into a larger pattern of anxiety among white Protestants over their cultural and economic differences with newer arrivals to America. This anxiety combined with superior political power allowed them to impose social engineering on immigrant populations.

By the mid-twentieth century, though, adoption had evolved into an institution designed as much to help childless couples as to help secure better homes for children. The supply of babies (and adopting couples much prefer infants) came mostly from unwed mothers and divorced households. If the birth parents were married, the law usually required the consent of both mother and father. If the birth parents were not married, the law usually did not require the genetic father's consent or made it easy to list him as unknown.

In part to protect the privacy interests of both the birth mother and the adoptive parents, and in part to keep the child from feeling pulled in different directions, secrecy was a hallmark of most adoptions in the twentieth century. The birth mother would work either with a private, often religious, agency or with a state agency to prepare to put the child up for adoption. The private or state agency would locate a prospective couple to adopt the child. The birth mother and the adoptive couple rarely met each other and often were not given any information about each other. Formally, the birth mother would relinquish the child to the care of the agency and then the agency would sign over rights, in a judicial proceeding, to the adoptive parents. The adoption would not be final until a court had ruled that the relinquishment was valid and that the adoption was in the child's best interest. But this procedure did not involve direct contact between the adults.

For much of this time, the state was concerned with making sure that the birth mother was not coerced into or paid for relinquishing her parental rights. As much as the state wanted to help childless couples, it was not willing to sanction a market for babies, although some observers believed that the fee structures of private agencies resembled markets in some respects. The state vested the birth mother with authority to "back out" of adoption plans that she had made while pregnant if the birth of the child caused her a change of heart.

The concern over baby selling may explain why religious organizations always played such a substantial role in adoptions. The courts generally trusted religious agencies not to be motivated by profit, and they trusted them not to exploit the birth mother. Even with this trust, states have sought to protect a birth mother during her decision to relinquish her parental rights. No state considers a mother's consent valid if she signed it before birth unless she is given an opportunity to repudiate her decision after the birth. Most states require that a consent to adoption be signed at least three days after the birth of the child. This provision recognizes that the process of birth itself may be a life-altering experience and that mothers cannot give meaningful consent to relinquish a baby before the birth.

Consent procedures are very different for biological fathers. Most states do allow fathers to sign a valid consent pre-birth, though sometimes they have the right to revoke that consent post-birth. Most states have a provision allowing an adoption to go through if, 30 days after birth, the father has not come forward in some manner. After that 30-day window, his consent is not needed, whether or not he was aware of the pregnancy. A man who thinks he is a father may protect his rights by notifying a state paternity registry of a claim to any child born from a named woman, but he must act to do so. His rights are not an artifact of his biological link. Many people view this differential treatment of mothers and fathers as essential to ensuring safe and quick infant adoptions, because often it is very difficult to locate the birth father. They also view it as justified by the different commitments men and women have during pregnancy. Women commit by carrying the baby. Men may volunteer to commit, but they may also disappear. Nothing in the birth process demands a show of commitment from the father.

In the last 40 years, the legal procedures regulating parents' relinquishment of their parental rights have not changed significantly, but the practices and norms surrounding adoption have changed dramatically. First, and probably most important, there are fewer infants available for adoption. The decline in number of infants is attributable both to much more prevalent and reliable birth control and to the rising acceptability of unwed motherhood, particularly among white and middle-class people. Many mothers who would have felt shamed into putting a child up for adoption in the mid-twentieth century now feel comfortable raising the child on their own. Contrary to some popular beliefs, the legalization of abortion had only a minimal effect on the supply of infants available for adoption. It was widespread use of contraception combined with white middle-class mothers keeping their children, more than the termination of pregnancies, that led to the decrease in numbers of infants available for adoption.

Second, the norms surrounding unwed fatherhood have evolved as well. Aided perhaps by a series of decisions in the 1970s in which the Supreme Court recognized that unwed fathers have some rights as fathers, courts are much less likely to dismiss unwed fathers' claims as antithetical to a child's best interest.[19] If unwed fathers appear unwilling to relinquish consent today, courts ordinarily take their claims seriously.

Third, and related to the first two changes, international adoption has become much more prevalent. The more unwed mothers kept their children, the fewer healthy infant children were available for adoption domestically. The greater solicitude the law paid to unwed father's rights, the more insecure potential adoptive parents felt about whether the adoption would stay valid if the absent biological father had not consented. Therefore, adoptive couples in the United States now often let the law of other countries determine their parental status. Many more children still await adoption in the United States than there are families seeking children. But the majority of those children are older or have health problems, and many American families prefer international adoption of infants to adoption of older children in the United States.

The fourth change in U.S. adoption practice is that most adoptions today are *open adoptions*. This means that the birth mother plays a role in choosing the parents who will adopt her child. Ongoing communication between birth parent(s) and adoptive parent(s) is encouraged, not forbidden. Legally, the differences between open adoptions and traditional secret adoptions are not significant. Ordinarily the birth parents still relinquish all legal rights, and the adoptive parents assume all legal rights and obligations. But ideally in open adoptions the birth mother or parents can play some role in the child's life. Sometimes, the birth parent(s) and the adoptive parent(s) enter into some sort of written visitation agreement. For reasons we will explore fully in Chapter 4, traditional rules that would have barred a nonlegal (but genetically related) parent from having a legally enforceable relationship with the child are waning, and now many courts entertain requests for visitation if there is a colorable claim that it is in the child's best interest for the court to do so. As a consequence, the greater the role the birth parent(s) play in the child's life once the child is born, the greater the likelihood that they might be able to petition a court for an enforceable visitation right, regardless of whether there is a formal agreement. Courts are careful to protect adoptive parents generally, so the past practices of the adoptive family toward the birth parent may be important to any grant of visitation.

The legal formalities associated with adoption have significant personal and social meaning in the situations just described, in which new parents adopt an infant whom they previously did not know. But the majority of adoptions do not involve the law making strangers into a family. Most adoptions involve the law giving somewhat more formal sanction to a parenting relationship that already exists. Most adoptions are either stepparent or foster parent adoptions, and they involve children the adoptive parent has already parented, not babies. Nonetheless, the legal requirements of adoption are the same. That is, the original parents, despite their established relationship to the child, must relinquish their parental rights. This can be difficult. With foster parent adoptions, the state usually has to terminate an unconsenting parent's rights. With step-parent adoptions, a custodial parent usually wants a new spouse to adopt, but the noncustodial parent can resist. In these cases, the concern is not that a vulnerable, new parent has been coerced into relinquishing rights by consent but that an established, but possibly wayward, parent is being usurped as parent over his or her objection.

The state must offer clear and convincing evidence of parental abuse or neglect before it can sever a parent's rights without the parent's consent (see Chapter 4). As a result, foster children are often at least several years old before they are eligible for adoption. This delay makes it harder to find parents willing to adopt and has created a critically high number of children needing homes relative to the number of families willing to adopt them. In response to the number of foster children in need of permanent adoption, most states have loosened their requirements for adoptive parents considerably. Fifty years ago, states and adoption agencies required adopters to be married, economically secure, and not too old. Today, states often allow single adults, openly gay couples, and grandparents to adopt. This vastly expanded class of people eligible to adopt is in part a function of necessity, because state agencies have so many children in need of placement. But it is also a function of expanded understandings of what constitutes good parenting. The more that single parents, gay parents, and grandparents model good parenting, the more arbitrary class, age, and sexual orientation qualifications are likely to seem.

In the hands of religious adoption agencies, matching of birth mother and adoptive parent religions was a common practice. At times, this "matching" was nothing more than pretense, because the birth mother may have sought the easiest, most generous agency, not the agency of her own religious tradition. As a condition of using that agency, she may have stated a desire for a religious match because it was a quid pro quo for services. While the practice of religious matching has loosened, it has not entirely disappeared, and policies in favor of religious matching still exist in a number of states.

A more controversial history attends the matching of adoptive parents and adoptive babies by race, particularly as between African Americans and whites. Race matching had been the historical practice in an era when adoption was secretive, and every attempt was made to create the illusion that an adopted child had been born to her adoptive parents. During the civil rights era of the 1960s, this practice relaxed somewhat, as white families in particular began adopting African American infants. In the 1970s, in response to severe criticism from the National Association of Black Social Workers (NABSW), this practice stopped for a time almost completely. The NABSW believed that interracial adoption deprived African American children of a positive racial identity, removed African American children from their rightful communities, and diverted attention from the devastating economic conditions in African American communities that caused African American babies to be relinquished for adoption in the first place. The NABSW also pointed out that the interracial adoption was never color-blind, as white children were not placed with African American families. The impact of the NABSW was profound, and interracial adoption has been fraught with controversy ever since. The number of African American children awaiting adoption exceeds the number of African Americans seeking to adopt, despite the higher rates of adoption per family among African Americans. This is particularly the case with older children or children with disabilities; placement of healthy infants is easy regardless of race matching practices.

Proponents of transracial adoption argue that children in need of adoption should never be denied a family or encounter delay because of their race or that of an otherwise qualified family, that the experience of racial identity is not uniformly shared, and that the ideals of integration should extend to the intimate circumstances of family connection.

The federal government has stepped in twice to encourage relaxation of race-matching practices, by prohibiting states from delaying an adoption in order to achieve a racial match.[20] These acts have not prohibited race-matching entirely, nor required race-blind placement. They have attempted to prevent delay of placements caused by the search for a race match. At the agency level it is difficult to police the role race is playing in a placement, given that it is still a permissible factor. Agencies that believe in race-matching can achieve it under federal law so long as they do not deny an adoption on grounds of race alone. But the federal legislation has moderated the consensus among social workers about the practice and has thereby relaxed the practice somewhat.

These federal interventions into race-matching practices are ironic, given that the other major federal intervention into adoption policies involved protecting the tribal identity of Native American children with the Indian Child Welfare Act of 1978 (ICWA). In response to concern from many Indian tribes that Indian children were being adopted off of Indian reservations and into non-Indian homes in alarming numbers, Congress passed the ICWA, vesting tribal courts with jurisdiction for all proceedings concerning Indian children domiciled on an Indian reservation. The act was explicit in its purpose of helping Indian tribes maintain cultural and social identity by rearing Indian children in Indian culture.

The contrasting treatment of African American and Indian children can be justified, legally, because Indian tribes have separate sovereignty in America and African Americans do not. Still, the contrasting treatment reflects different approaches to the legitimacy of viewing children as having a core ethnic identity. Moreover, these regulations suggest that the state is not only free to determine who parents are, it can actively shape how children identify themselves.

Notwithstanding congressional reticence to permit racial matching in the non-Indian context, most adoption agencies across the country do use race as a factor in placing children, preferring a match where all others things are equal. White families wishing to adopt children of any race other than their own are generally asked to demonstrate their ability to nurture a positive racial identity in a child. This is ordinarily achieved by showing racial integration in their lives and an understanding of the challenges facing minority children. Meanwhile, an enormous number of international adoptions are in fact interracial and meet with little controversy on that ground.

The most controversial form of adoption today is the inaptly named *second-parent adoption*. This label applies to a second adult seeking to adopt a child who already has one parent of the same gender. Requests for second-parent adoptions usually come from one gay parent who is either the biological parent of the child (often by means of artificial insemination, so there is no other parent) or the single adoptive parent of a child. In either case, the parties ask the court to declare parenthood in another adult without relinquishing anyone's parental rights. Because both adoption and reproductive technologies allow the existence of just one parent, second-parent adoptions are the one example of adoptions that do not involve the termination of anyone else's parental rights. But they do require a court to acknowledge that a child has two mothers or two fathers. Second parent adoptions are available in approximately half of the states today and can be an essential source of parental rights for same sex parents living in a state that does not recognize civil unions or same sex marriage.

3. Technological Reproduction

Many would-be parents who were unsuccessful trying to get pregnant once had adoption as their only choice. Today they may turn to reproductive technology specialists to aid them in their quest to be parents. Most people using advanced reproductive technologies are married couples trying to produce children with their own genetic material in their own bodies. Couples who fertilize their own eggs and sperm outside the womb and then insert the fertilized egg back in the woman's womb present no issue for the law of parenthood. Parenthood is determined just as it would be if they had become pregnant in a more conventional way.[21] For many potential parents, however, this is not an option.

Sometimes a woman's eggs are too old or simply not capable of accepting certain sperm. Sometimes a man's sperm are not strong enough to fertilize an egg. Sometimes the process of gestation would put the potential mother at grave risk of injury. Sometimes a lesbian couple needs to use someone else's sperm. Sometimes a gay male couple needs to use someone else's eggs and gestational labor. Sometimes a single person wants to parent his or her own genetic issue. As long as any of these potential parents live in or have the resources to travel to states that permit the procedures and contracts involved, they can now create children for whom they will be considered parents.

The least controversial and oldest form of reproductive technology is sperm donation. Indeed, to call sperm donation a technology may elevate it too much. Many babies have been produced, without the aid of any doctor or specialist, by people who figured out a reliable way to arrange insemination informally with a turkey baster. For people who want something more formal, doctors specializing in obstetrics or infertility will aid in the insemination process, and sperm can be reliably purchased from a number of national sperm banks. Most states have statutes that name as the father the husband of a woman who gives birth to a child after being artificially inseminated with someone else's sperm, if that insemination was performed by a licensed physician. The sperm donor signs a release absolving himself of any rights or responsibilities for any child produced. He is paid a modest amount for his services.

In the United States, unlike many other countries in which sperm donation is common, men may donate sperm anonymously. This means that a child may never be able to locate his or her genetic father. Such a child is similar to other children who never know their genetic fathers, whether adopted, born to unwed mothers, born to married mothers whose husbands left, or born to married mothers who keep a secret. But in cases of artificial insemination, the parents know from the outset that the genetic father will not be known. There are no reliable statistics kept on how many children are born each year using donated sperm. Experts believe that the number has grown significantly in recent years. It has grown because more people are aware of sperm donation and because some states have lessened restrictions on whom sperm banks can sell to and whom doctors can inseminate. But much of this area has always been unregulated. Many states never thought to bar single women from going to sperm banks, because 40 years ago single women did not go to sperm banks. It was not the law that served as a barrier but social norms with regard to single and gay parenthood.

Today, both single women and lesbian couples buy sperm from sperm banks. This means that there are now numerous children born into families that never intend to have a father. Parentage in these cases is fairly noncontroversial, mostly because none of the relevant parties have an interest in challenging it: The woman who became pregnant is the uncontested mother of the child, and the the genetic father has no interest in the child. If the birth mother has a partner, that partner may become a parent by virtue of a second-parent adoption (in some places) or try to secure visitation rights by signing a parenting agreement with the birth mother (see visitation discussion). In the states that recognize civil unions or same sex marriage, same sex partners may be presumed to be parents of their partner's biological children.

When single women or lesbian couples acquire sperm from a donor known to them personally, parentage can be more complicated. Some potential mothers prefer to use a known donor. They may wish to screen or control for genetics more personally, they may wish to find a donor with a genetic connection to a same sex co-parent so that the child will be a blood relative of both same sex parents, or they may wish to preserve an informal and limited role for that donor in the child's life. When they do know the donor, they often do not sign legal documents delineating parental rights and responsibilities. Even if the parties draft such documents, courts do not always honor them if the documents do not conform to the statutory requirements for relinquishing parental rights. For instance, relinquishment of paternal rights in the adoption context usually requires that a new parent be willing to assume the obligation of father. When a sperm donor agrees to relinquish his parental rights, he often does so without a waiting parent ready to take his place.

When parentage is challenged in cases like this, most courts have used a *preconception intent* standard to determine parental status. If the parties intended for the sperm donor to retain a role as father, the court will afford the sperm donor parental rights. If the parties did not so intend, then courts will not. Discerning preconception intent is not always easy, particularly if the parties behavior since the child was born seems inconsistent with that intent. If the sperm donor assumes an active role in the child's life, courts are more likely to afford him some sort of parental right, regardless of what the original agreement was. In this sense, known sperm donors get treated like birth parents in the adoption context. Their genetic connection in and of itself may not get them relationship rights, but if coupled with an ongoing relationship with the child, courts are more likely to afford them some rights. If there is little contact with the child once born, courts rely on preconception intent.

This intent standard for determining legal parenthood formally applies only to reproductive technology cases. If a single woman wants to get pregnant using a known man's sperm and does so conventionally by having sex with him, preconception intent is entirely irrelevant. The man need not be aware that she is trying to get pregnant. She can lie to him about her intent, her birth control method, or her plans to sue him in paternity. He can even be underage, and she guilty of statutory rape. If she delivers a child, and wants to name him as the father, or if he wants to be the father, and either can prove it genetically, the law makes him the father (as long as she is not married to someone else). No one's preconception "intent" will matter. Yet, if the woman uses somewhat less conventional, but not particularly intricate, methods of sperm collection and insemination, then preconception intent governs the paternity question.

This "intent" standard when using reproductive technologies is certainly useful to institutions, such as research hospitals, that invest in research and facilities to assist infertile individuals. It gives potential parents some degree of assurance that their parental rights will be secure if their expensive investment in reproductive technology proves fruitful. But it also shows that the state continues to be confused about why and when genetic connection should determine parenthood. In addition, the intent standard puts pressure on the two-parent normative family because one person can intend to be a parent by him- or herself.

The intent standard governs in those situations involving more complicated reproductive technologies as well. There are no national egg banks, the way there are sperm banks, but egg donation is now fairly commonplace, with intending parents often advertising for and sometimes interviewing the woman whose eggs they will use. Eggs are significantly more expensive than sperm, and for good reason: They are much harder to get, and the process of getting them is much more taxing on the donor. Once eggs are harvested, the intending parents inseminate them (usually with the sperm of the intending father) and place them in the womb of the intending mother (although a gestational surrogate can be used as well — see below). The egg donor, like the sperm donor, signs an agreement releasing her from all rights and responsibilities with regard to any child produced. The purchasers of the eggs become the legal parents and may or may not decide to have further contact with the egg donor.

Although unnerving to some, egg and sperm donation are not particularly controversial, perhaps because sperm donation has been around, in some form, for so long. The Catholic Church and some other religious groups are opposed to any nonnatural reproductive processes, but most of the controversy surrounding the commercialization of reproduction has been generated by the selling of women's gestational labor, not the selling of genetic material.

When surrogacy was introduced, the surrogate was paid for both her egg and her gestational labor. In the early and famous *Baby M* case, for instance, the intended father's sperm was injected into the surrogate who then carried the child to term. The surrogate was both the genetic and gestational mother of the child. When the child was born, the surrogate mother did not want to relinquish her parental rights, as the surrogacy contract had contemplated. In a well-publicized decision, the New Jersey Supreme Court refused to enforce the surrogacy contract, finding that it did not provide enough of the procedural safeguards normally involved in ensuring that a parent's rights were being properly terminated.[22] The court cited requirements that states must prove parents unfit before terminating parental rights and adoption statutes outlining the procedures that mothers must go through before relinquishing consent — *after* the child has been born. In *Baby M*, the court decided that the child's legal parents were the surrogate mother and the intended father, who was the sperm provider and married to a different woman with whom he intended to raise the child. The father was awarded custody of the baby, with liberal visitation to her biological mother.

Traditional surrogacy contracts like the one involved in *Baby M* are now rare. Most people who need to use a surrogate usually sign a contract that involves just the surrogate's gestational labor, not her genetic material. Intending couples either use their own egg (maybe fertilized with their own sperm) or they use sperm and egg purchased elsewhere and pay a surrogate to carry the fertilized egg to term. The surrogate delivers a baby to whom she has no genetic connection, which eliminates one major source of her potential claim.

Not all states enforce gestational surrogacy contracts. A few states even outlaw the practice, but enough states accommodate them for their prevalence to have grown substantially. In truth, we do not know how many states will enforce these contracts because the vast majority are never challenged. The parties comply with the contract as written. Most lawyers write a surrogacy agreement such that the law of a state thought to be sympathetic to the procedure will govern in case of a challenge. In one landmark case of a gestational surrogacy contract that was challenged, the California Supreme Court ruled that the parties' preconception intent is what should determine parenthood.[23] That preconception intent was found in the contract. Comparably, in cases that are not challenged, the parties' intent as manifested in the contract and their subsequent behavior determines legal parenthood. Thus, parenthood in the gestational surrogacy context is determined as it is in the donated gamete context, by intent.

The intent standard for determining parenthood cannot be easily reconciled with paternity doctrine, the purpose of which has always been to make unwilling men into legal fathers. The intent standard acknowledges the legitimacy of a single-parent family, and it suggests that planning, not fortuity or marriage, should determine legal parenthood. One reason courts may be sympathetic to the intent standard in the reproductive technology area is that, in contrast to most paternity cases, child support is rarely an issue. Most reproductive technologies are expensive. Those with access to the services usually have the resources to support the child.

There is growing debate about the importance of genetic connection, however. This debate may jeopardize the intent standard. The open adoption movement, active in this country since the 1970s, and the growing movement to ban anonymous gamete donation so that a child can locate his or her genetic parents reflect belief in the power and importance of genetics in families. There are also medical reasons for access to genetic information. The medical justification may grow less persuasive as genetic science makes it increasingly possible to predict and treat based on the presenting DNA. Nonetheless, for countless disorders that are not yet accurately mapped to DNA, the simplest and best prediction of many routine diseases and medical disorders remains a family history, and genetic tests for diseases remain so expensive that they are not offered as routine medical screening.

Meanwhile, the psychological arguments for genetic knowledge are growing louder. Some argue that children who cannot locate their genetic parents feel psychologically lost. Others argue that knowing one's genetic roots is an essential part of healthy identity formation. Nearly constant social reference to who a child "takes after" or to the source of a child's various traits can be a significant source of discomfort to a growing child. Some people simply believe that curiosity about genetics is inevitable and therefore the law should facilitate children's ability to find genetic parents. At the same time, history makes clear that legal parenthood has never mapped entirely onto genetic parenthood. Sometimes children were aware that their legal parents were not their genetic parents; sometimes they were not. We have no good evidence about how much that knowledge has mattered to the children's well-being. But a growing number of people believe that it has.

4. Constitutional Parenthood

In addition to the state rules determining parenthood, there is a constitutional law of parental status as well. On several different occasions, the Supreme Court has been asked to determine whether the Constitution protects a genetic father's right to legal parental status.[24] No mother has ever made a comparable claim, presumably because the fit between the state law of motherhood and genetic connection has been much stronger.

Taken together, the opinions indicate that the constitution does not protect a right to parental status based on genetic paternity alone. The constitutional paternal status cases suggest that the state has some duty to afford a genetic father an opportunity to come forward to claim parental status, but the state is not compelled to expend effort to find the genetic father. Statutes that require a mother's but not a father's post-birth consent to adoption have never been successfully challenged under the U.S. Constitution. A state is free to vest parental status in the mother's husband (the marital presumption) even if the genetic father has a relationship with the child. The government is also free to vest citizenship in the foreign-born children of genetic American mothers without necessarily vesting it in the foreign-born children of genetic American fathers, because mothers and fathers are thought to have different relationships to the child at birth.[25] If the genetic father has developed a relationship with the growing child, however, and especially if no other man has been serving as a presumptive father, then the state may at least be compelled to treat father and mother comparably. Positive parental actions on a father's part are needed to create a claim equal to what a mother gains by virtue of her substantial gestational contribution.

The constitutional trope for explaining this differential treatment of genetic mothers and fathers comes from equal protection doctrine, which requires that men and women be treated the same only when they are similarly situated. The Court has made clear on several occasions that at birth mothers and fathers are not similarly situated because they did not share in the gestational process. Gestation gives a genetic mother a greater constitutional claim to parenthood than a genetic father has. As the child grows, however, if the genetic mother and father share the parenting roles, then the mother's relative greater commitment to the child wanes in proportion to the father's. At some point, if both have served as parents, they are entitled to equal treatment as parents. So it is relationship, in addition to genetic connection, that is necessary to secure constitutional protection as a parent. This is not to say that all statutes must treat men and women differently at birth, but only that the U.S. Constitution does not prohibit states from doing so.

Some students of equal protection law are surprised at this overtly different treatment of men and women. But people familiar with the totality of the state law of parenthood rarely are. Motherhood and fatherhood have always been determined differently. Perhaps because we never knew paternal genetic connection with certainty, or perhaps because the law wanted to put a premium on stability in relationships, the law has always needed presumptions of fatherhood in ways that it did not think it needed presumptions of motherhood.

What would it mean to have comparable legal presumptions govern for both mothers and fathers? Maternal and paternal status could be presumed from the fact of having acted as parent or the fact of having signed the birth certificate. Or, we could have a licensing process for parental status, just as we have one for marital status. Whether those presumptions would be rebuttable or those licenses rendered void with contradicting genetic evidence would be a question of policy: Who do we want the parents to be? A regime like this would probably be difficult for many people to accept because it would so disrupt the common understanding that parenthood is a pre-legal genetic fact. Allegiance to that prelegal view of parenthood, however, requires taking into account biological differences in the reproductive process. Taking account of those differences, in turn, leads to different legal treatment of women and men in ways that seem at odds with gender equality doctrine.

This tension extends through the law of adoption. A true equality-preferencing regime would probably afford both fathers and mothers substantial protection to ensure that they were fully aware of the gravity of relinquishing parental rights. Currently, the law is primarily concerned that birth mothers' relinquishment of parental rights be carefully regulated because what she is giving up is so important. The difference in treatment also reflects the accurate belief that genetic fathers are much more likely to abandon their genetic issue than are genetic mothers. But the law could afford comparable protection to fathers. Both could be required to relinquish rights post-birth. A rule requiring more procedural protections for genetic fathers would upset infant adoption and child welfare advocates concerned about the lives of older children unable to be adopted for want of a father's permission. Tracking down an absent or unidentified father adds time and requires resources that child welfare agencies would prefer to direct to the care of children. These are powerful policy considerations that counsel against treating mothers and fathers comparably. But a very strong allegiance to equal treatment of the sexes could trump those policy considerations.

One area where the law has not treated men and women differently is in determining parental status in cases involving reproductive technology. For the most part, preconception intent governs, regardless of who is genetically connected or who gave what gestational labor (the *Baby M* situation being the one, mostly obsolete, exception). The facts on the ground hardly suggest gender equality, however. Eggs are much more expensive than sperm. Gestational labor cannot be sold by men. In the area in which the market controls, it is all too obvious why men and women, mothers and fathers would be treated differently. They are treated differently because their biological contributions to the creation of children are so different. The law of parental status has not treated men and women differently solely because men and women play different socially constructed roles, although that certainly is a factor. The law of parental status has treated men and women differently in part because biology assigns them different roles in the birth process. Whether the law should care about those different biological roles and whether the law has created more gender distinctions than it needs to based on those biological roles are perfectly valid policy questions. But history shows that the law always has accepted disparity and still does confer motherhood and fatherhood differently.

ENDNOTES

1. The California legislature created a status called "domestic partnership" that was a limited grant of rights but later amended it so that it was the full legal equivalent of marriage for state law purposes. The state was conferring domestic partnership status on same sex couples when the California Supreme Court ruled in June of 2008 that same sex couples were entitled to the institution of marriage. In November of 2008, voters prohibited same sex couples in California from marrying, presumably returning the law to its prior state of robust domestic partnership. Every other jurisdiction that uses the term *domestic partnership* uses it to confer a status that includes only some but not all the legal rights and obligations of marriage.

2. 18 Cal. 3d 660 (1976).

3. *Braschi v. Stahl Associates*, 74 N.Y.2d 201 (1989).

4. 388 U.S. 1 (1967).

5. *Perez v. Sharpe*, 32 Cal. 2d 711 (Cal. 1948).

6. *Zablocki v. Redhail*, 434 U.S. 374 (1978).

7. *Turner v. Safley*, 482 U.S. 78 (1987).

8. His conviction was upheld on appeal to the Utah Supreme Court, 2004 Ut. 76 (2004).

9. *Baehr v. Lewin*, 74 Haw. 530 (1993).

10. *Baker v. Vermont*, 170 Vt. 194 (1999).

11. 798 N.E.2d 941 (Mass. 2003).

12. In 2000, Proposition 22 was passed in California, defining marriage as an institution between a man and a woman. In 2003, the California legislature expanded the state's domestic partnership law to provide the same state law benefits as marriage.

13. *Lewis v. Harris*, 908 A2d 196 (NJ 2006).

14. *In re Marriage Cases*, 43 Cal 4th 757 (2008).

15. *Kerrigan v. Commissioner of Public Health*, 289 Conn. 135 (2008).

16. 1 U.S.C. Sec. 7 and 28 U.S.C. Sec. 1738(c).

17. The one exception to this non-access rule was in cases in which the husband was "beyond the four seas" of England.

18. *Michael H. v Gerald D.*, 491 U.S. 110 (1989).

19. *Stanley v. Illinois*, 405 U.S. 645 (1972); *Quilloin v. Walcott*, 434 U.S. 246 (1978); *Caban v. Mohammed*, 463 U.S. 248 (1983); *Lehr v. Robertson*, 463 U.S. 248 (1983).

20. Multi-Ethnic Placement Act, 42 U.S.C. 622 (1994), amended 1996 (Interethnic Adoption Provisions).

21. However, controversies can arise if, before the fertilized egg is implanted in the wife's womb, the couple divorces or one party dies. At that point, the law has to decide who has the authority to implant or dispose of the fertilized eggs. Usually the law allows the person who does not want to produce children to block the procreation.

22. *In the Matter of Baby M*, 109 N.J. 396 (1988).

23. *Johnson v. Calvert*, 19 Cal. Rptr. 2d 494 (1993) (en banc).

24. *Stanley v. Illinois*, 405 U.S. 645 (1972); *Quilloin v. Walcott*, 434 U.S. 246 (1978); *Caban v. Mohammed*, 463 U.S. 248 (1983); *Lehr v. Robertson*, 463 U.S. 248 (1983).

25. *Miller v. Albright*, 523 U.S. 420 (1998); *Nguyen v. INS*, 533 U.S. 53 (2001).

～ 3 ～

Legal Interaction with Ongoing Families

We have seen that family ties are formed in a variety of ways — through licenses, informal practices, intentional acts, agreements, accidents, legal fictions, genetic connections, and technological interventions. The law acts in various ways around family formation. But what happens once family ties are formed and before they are broken? In other words, what are the *consequences* of the legal recognition of existing relationships? This chapter reviews how the law regulates or refuses to regulate families between formation and dissolution or death. This we call the *law of the ongoing family*.

A. ONGOING FAMILY: THE MARITAL RELATIONSHIP

Three important concepts govern the ongoing marital relationship at common law. First, a tradition of legal nonintervention in marriages remains salient in today's doctrine, although it has never been absolute in practice. Second, the historical view that marriage merged the parties into one person, termed coverture (for the husband's "cover" of the wife), led to a series of special doctrines relating to spouses, a number of which are still reflected in modern law. Finally, at common law husbands owed their wives a duty of support during marriage, and wives owed their husbands a reciprocal duty of service. Those duties are the basis of a number of still existing doctrines.

For much of U.S. history, until the no-fault divorce reform of the 1960s and 1970s, divorce was not easily obtained. For some individuals, such as those who had committed adultery or engaged in other marital fault, it was not available at all. Under that regime, it was possible for couples to be living together or apart in tension or disharmony but with every expectation of a continuing marriage. Today's student needs to understand that more inescapable version of marriage to understand the common law rules associated with married couples.

1. Nonintervention

The common view is that not much happens between marriages and the law as long as the marriage is harmonious. During a marriage, there is a notion, if not a rock-solid doctrine, of nonintervention. This "transactional" view of the relationship between law and families — that law shows up at the moments of transaction at the beginning of a marriage and again at the end — is reflected in both constitutional law and in state common law practices. It is not an accurate view of how the law relates to married couples. But the persistence of the idea in spite of its inaccuracy necessitates an elaboration of it before we turn to the interesting ways in which it breaks down.

There are a number of doctrines where we see the nonintervention principle play out, often combined with the other principles governing the ongoing marriage. Rather than look at them chronologically, let's take them from benign to malignant, to better understand the way nonintervention operates.

In 1965, the United States Supreme Court decided *Griswold v. Connecticut*.[1] This is a giant among landmark Supreme Court cases because it knits together the "penumbras" from several rights in the Constitution to elaborate a *right of privacy* that would go on to be the source of the right in *Roe v. Wade*,[2] among other cases. But the actual dispute in *Griswold* was over criminalizing the use of contraception by a married couple. The opinion stakes out the privacy right from state interference in large part on the basis of nonintervention into marriage as a principle. In other words, as articulated in *Griswold* and played out in other constitutional marriage cases at the state and federal level, the married couple is unified in a desire to prevent the state from interfering with decisions the couple makes about their marriage. *Griswold*'s nonintervention, then, is a doctrine that supports the desires of married people to carve out a government-free sphere within their marriage. It draws its intuitive antistatist support from common law strands of nonintervention in marriage.

As we will explore in greater detail later in this chapter, married couples have an obligation during a marriage to provide support to one another. That support was traditionally interpreted as financial support from husbands to wives — or provision of basic necessities such as housing, food, and clothing. From wives to husbands, that support was interpreted at common law to be an obligation of service, primarily of labor. In 1953, the Nebraska Supreme Court decided a case that demonstrated a different side of the nonintervention doctrine. In *McGuire v. McGuire*,[3] a wife brought an action against her husband, with whom she still lived in marriage, for failing to live up to his support obligations. The case details his stinginess (their house has no running water, he does not buy her new clothing, and so forth). The court criticizes his frugality but finds that her only remedy for nonsupport is to file for divorce or legal separation. She cannot bring a nonsupport action while she is still married and living with him, because of the nonintervention doctrine. Here we have a support doctrine intended to place obligations on the husband but with no available enforcement by the wife during an ongoing marriage. The court spells out her method of enforcing that support obligation, and it is through ending the marriage.

To some this case represents one of the benefits of marriage, which is some form of unity of two individuals into one unit. That benefit comes at the cost of giving up such individual rights as pursuing lawsuits against one another. Others will point out that given the tremendous diversity in spending among families and the absence of a comprehensible and widely applicable standard for support, litigating the appropriate award would be very difficult — although family law is full of such discretionary decision-making.

You will also hear this doctrine defended on the grounds that a court's willingness to decide financial disputes between married couples would open the floodgates to constant litigation on the one hand and sow the seeds of marital discord on the other. Most commentators accept those as legitimate reasons to deny a remedy in this sort of case. Indeed, some see this kind of court opinion as marriage respecting, in much the way *Griswold* is marriage respecting.

Scrutinize the arguments, though. Are married couples across the United States seeking to remain married yet resolve their disputes in court? In other words, is rejection of a remedy the reason spouses don't sue each other in the ongoing marriage? Does the nonintervention doctrine itself really explain the absence of these suits, rather than the rarity of the desire to remain married but sue your spouse? One might think that when a marriage's internal negotiations have so broken down that a court order is sought, it would ordinarily be a divorce action. The floodgates argument anticipates a universe of marital disputes that couples would choose to bring to a court. But it is difficult to find cases raising the *McGuire* issue. This is probably not because the law is so well settled, but rather because it is the rare spouse who wants to remain married to someone with whom they also wish to litigate disputes. The floodgates argument advanced by courts is probably not terribly well considered.

The idea that this opinion respects marital privacy is also shaky. In *Griswold*, the couple as a unit asked for privacy from state intervention. In *McGuire*, one party to the marriage invited the state in. Respecting the privacy of the other spouse is different than respecting the privacy of the marriage — it is imposing nonintervention over the objections of one half of the marriage. Finally, there is concern that state intervention will sow the seeds of discord in a marriage. Like the floodgates argument, this idea avoids the level of discord that must already exist for Mrs. McGuire to have brought her claim in the first place.

This critique is not a call for *McGuire*-type lawsuits; indeed, the universe of possible *McGuire* suits may be vanishingly small: Today those inclined to bring their marriage to court want a divorce and can get one far more easily than could Mrs. McGuire. Rather, our analysis is an illustration of the operation of the nonintervention doctrine. The marriage-supporting reasoning for the doctrine is as much rationalization by legal actors as real motivation. The motivation for the doctrine may also include an aversion to knowing and exposing the bad as well as the good that occurs inside marriages. In other words, it may be a doctrine that protects the courts' sensibilities more than its dockets. In this sense it is ideological, rooted in the desire not to hear evidence that contradicts harmonious depictions of ongoing marriages.

Moving from marriage-protective through marriage-neutral applications of nonintervention in ongoing marriages, we arrive at clearly destructive incarnations of the concept: nonintervention in family violence. The nonintervention principle is evident in the marital rape exemption. At common law, a husband could not be guilty of raping his wife. Here, the principles of coverture (that they are one unit), reciprocal obligations (that she owes him a duty of services), and nonintervention (that the law has no place in the ongoing interactions of spouses), came together with toxic force to authorize the imposition of unwanted sexual contact without fear of reprisal from the state.

A reform movement over the past several decades has led to the modification of this doctrine in every state. But those modifications rarely amount to a complete elimination of the distinction between marital and nonmarital rape. Instead, courts and legislatures struggle with the contours of the marital rape exemption in the belief that some higher level of violence or faster complaint, for example, are needed before it is justified for the state to step in when the parties are married to one another.

A moment's reflection exposes the absurdity of respecting marriage by allowing rape within it, yet the doctrinal struggles may again suggest legal aversion to unveiling the dark side of some marriages. The persistence of marital rape categories partially reflects concern that in the heat of a divorce, angry women will bring rape charges against their soon-to-be ex-spouse. Why are legal actors so averse to those charges being brought, though, given how difficult they are to prove? It is very difficult to prove rape without evidence of physical injury in a situation in which the parties had previously had consensual sex. The marital rape exception probably serves more as a barrier to evidence of the parties' sexual history being introduced than as protection against conviction. This would suggest again that courts are reticent even to hear evidence of extreme marital conflict.

The history of domestic violence intervention suggests a comparable but somewhat distinct dynamic between the law and the marital unit. At common law, physical discipline was a right of husbands against their wives and children. Even as that stance became the subject of criticism and reform from the

1970s onward, a regime developed for managing intimate violence that diverged from the handling of violence between those who were not in intimate relationships.

Those separate legal regimes addressing domestic violence exist to varying degrees almost everywhere in the United States today and involve a variety of different strategies. These include restraining orders against abusers, mandatory arrest policies, required counseling for abusers, victimless prosecutions, and shelters for victims. These programs have brought much needed relief to many battered women. The frequency with which courts now issue temporary restraining orders, which a woman can get without her abuser appearing in court and which can prevent a man from entering their common home or seeing his children, suggests a dramatic shift away from rigid notions of coverture and marital privacy. There is no doubt that many prosecutors and judges take domestic violence much more seriously than they did 30 or 40 years ago.

But problems persist. Conviction rates are low. Deterrence programs often do not work. Victims return to their abusers. And victims are killed — with astounding frequency. Some of the law's failure in this area can be attributed to traditional judicial reticence to wade through the intimate details of a couple's life, even if there has been severe violence. Judges and law enforcement have been taught that law and social norms honor family privacy. The more often a couple breaks up and reconciles, the more a court may feel it is interfering with a marriage, not adjudicating a claim of battery. It is a court's responsibility to do both in cases of domestic violence. But judges are uncomfortable doing the former. Moreover, because the victim and the perpetrator are members of a family, judges and prosecutors and sometimes the parties themselves may believe that counseling or a severe warning or scolding will be enough to curb the violence. Often it is not.

The problems with eradicating or even controlling domestic violence run deeper, though. Victims often recant or cease to cooperate with the prosecution because they are, like many people in families, economically and emotionally dependent, in these cases on their abusers. The victim may fear the abuser too much to follow through on a criminal complaint. If she forgives him, wants to love him, and believes (usually mistakenly) that the violence will stop, it is hard for the state to proceed with a successful prosecution because her testimony may be compromised. Just as important, the pathology that grips many abusers often transcends normal criminal behavior. Fueled by the emotion that is supposed to keep families together but can also turn deadly, abusers pursue their victims relentlessly and irrationally. If there is not enough evidence to keep such abusers in jail, the law has difficulty stopping them. Even if courts were willing to condemn domestic violence claims as they condemn standard batteries, it is not clear that willingness alone would be enough to curb the cycles of irrational and therefore difficult-to-deter violence that plagues many violent relationships.

2. Coverture

At common law in the United States through much of the nineteenth century, a woman's legal status changed dramatically by virtue of being married. The concept of coverture prevailed, merging the wife's legal identity into that of the husband. The law recognized her only through him — only he could make contracts involving her, control her real and personal property, and "discipline" her physically. She was "covered" by him. He did not take title to her real property, but he had the right to use, manage, and convey it, while she had no rights of management, income, or control. Coverture operated at the formal level by merging the two people into the husband, and the logic of that formality dictated many of its legal consequences. For example, spouses could not sue one another in tort, because they were one person, and that would mean suing yourself. A woman could not be made to testify against her husband because it would require her to testify against herself. He could not commit a crime against her, for the same reason. The legal fiction of marriage as the unity of spouses into the husband defined the legal landscape.

Coverture was thrown out in a series of reforms beginning in the nineteenth century. Those reforms were to both laws governing marriage in particular and to laws pertaining to women more generally. No court would argue today that there are legitimate remnants of coverture remaining. Yet many doctrines that arose because of coverture and were originally justified by the logic of coverture remain in place, with some modernizations, to this day. In the cases where the doctrine still lives, the *justification* for the doctrine has changed in light of the disfavor cast over coverture. By changing the reasoning for certain doctrines, the law of the family has managed to preserve some of the attributes of coverture through to present times. A few examples will suffice to explain this phenomenon.

Tort Law Immunity. As one example, at common law spouses were immune from tort liability to each other. Because a person could not sue himself, the thinking went, it made no sense for one spouse to sue another, because the law had unified them into one person. In the modern era, courts and legislatures have chipped away at this tort immunity, so that it is gone completely for intentional torts and greatly diminished or eliminated for reckless and even negligent torts in most areas.

But some courts still preserve a role for immunity between spouses. New reasons have arisen, since coverture will no longer suffice to justify the rules. Instead, tort immunity is justified by the same concerns that drove the court in *McGuire v. McGuire* — concern over creating tension between spouses by countenancing a lawsuit. This justification might raise the same question: It is the rare harmonious spouse who would sue the other spouse in any way that would create dissension between them. The reason a harmonious spouse would sue in tort would be because he had purchased liability insurance to cover his accidents and wanted that insurance to be in effect even if the victim of that accident were his own spouse. For some courts, this has been a reason to maintain the tort immunity — to prevent fraudulent claims between collusive spouses. But other courts have felt it is the responsibility of the insurance carrier to exclude suits by spouses, and there is no fraud in the claims if the insurance company failed to exclude spouses when they sold the policy. To assume that it is fraud is to engage in the same presumption of unity that supported coverture.

Evidentiary Privileges. At common law, a wife could not testify against her husband. In a sense, it would violate the right not to incriminate oneself — coverture having merged the parties. As coverture has receded, courts have been more willing in some cases to allow the testimony of one spouse against another for what she observed (adverse testimony). But many jurisdictions are still reluctant, especially in criminal cases, to allow the testimony of one spouse against another about "confidential communications," meaning things they said to each other out of the presence of third parties. Many exceptions have developed even to this version of the rule, but the principle remains. Now the confidential communications rule is justified as a means of protecting the relationship between spouses — as a court-mandated sphere of "safe" communications for incriminating matters. A part of coverture has thus been converted to a doctrine that protects the sanctity of marriage.

3. Reciprocal Obligations: Service for Support

The third important principle governing ongoing marriages is the legally imposed duty of support each spouse has toward the other. At common law, this was a duty of husbands to support their wives, while wives had a duty of service to their husbands. In the modern era, these obligations remain, only each spouse owes both — a duty of support and services, and some states call both duties the *duty of support*. The *duty of services* meant that a wife owed her husband her labor, either outside the cash economy but in the household economy, or in the cash economy, with her wages owed directly to her husband. Earnings statutes in the late nineteenth century for the first time gave wives the right to contract with third parties for wages and keep those wages.

While a marriage is ongoing, the legal enforcement of this obligation is indirect at best. Recall that the nonintervention doctrine elaborated above precludes court enforcement of the support obligation by one spouse against the other in a direct action during the marriage. Understanding the areas where the support and service obligations might still come into play and when they might not is crucial to understanding the obligations themselves.

Before easily available divorce, the more common action was a civil support action, which allowed a couple to be separated but enforced the obligation of a husband to support his wife post-separation, because they were still married. These arrangements were routinely permanent and might look to an outsider like today's divorce. The alimony action, now termed maintenance, which occurs at divorce, is based on the support obligation, on the theory that the support obligation survives the divorce. In the modern era, there has been much debate and some transformation of that obligation as it is reflected in maintenance awards at divorce. Nonetheless, the support obligation has some ongoing relevance at divorce. But during marriage, it is enforced only through the rare criminal prosecution, the third-party *necessaries* action, and indirectly through restrictions on the ability to contract *out* of the obligation.

Criminal prosecutions for nonsupport can be brought under the narrowest of circumstances: when a spouse has deserted the other without divorce and left the other destitute, without shelter, food, or clothing. Nonsupport actions have more ongoing relevance with respect to child support than spousal obligations.

The most interesting mechanism for enforcing the support obligation during an ongoing marriage is the *doctrine of necessaries*. Under this doctrine, the wife at common law could purchase necessary items, such as food, clothing, or medical attention, from third parties on credit, and her husband would be obligated to pay her bills pursuant to his support duty. Practically speaking, the necessaries doctrine gave third parties the right to sue husbands as a means of enforcing the support obligation. He did not need to consent to or know about the purchases, so long as the items fell under his support obligation. A court would decide whether an item was "necessary" based on a husband's financial standing: The wealthier he was, the more items would be necessary for his wife. She could not sue him directly for support, but she could borrow to buy necessaries and have her creditor do so. However, if the husband had already supplied the items to his wife, then the third-party creditor could not recover against him. This made it a risk for a third party to extend credit to a wife in the hopes of recovering on this doctrine alone. In the era of gender-neutral marriage laws, with both spouses owing each other a duty of support, the necessaries doctrine has been enforced against either spouse equally. Some states have chosen to abolish the doctrine, but others retain it as a coherent extension of the duty of support.

Because creditors, in their self-interest, no longer routinely extend credit on the basis of marriage, the continued existence of the doctrine has few practical consequences. The one area where the doctrine of necessaries has real ongoing consequences concerns medical expenses. Several high-profile cases have held that a hospital may collect against one spouse for the other spouse's medical treatment, because the spouses owe each other a duty of support, and medical expenses are necessary. If one spouse's medical bills run into the hundreds of thousands, the impact of the necessaries doctrine is that the other spouse may not protect her assets from the devastating financial effects of her spouse's uninsured illness. This is true even if she explicitly refuses to assume financial responsibility for these debts in writing and in every way possible at the time the services are rendered.

Surely the oddest attribute of the necessaries doctrine is that it gives a third-party creditor a right to enforce an obligation between spouses that they have no right to enforce themselves. There is clear intervention, by an outsider, more intrusive it would seem than intervention when one spouse has petitioned for it. In other words, the outsider has a superior right to force redistribution within a marriage, in the guise of a duty that is unenforceable between the two spouses. Marital nonintervention was enough to prevent suit between spouses in *McGuire*, but it is not enough to prevent the suit of a third-party creditor. This shows nonintervention to be less marriage protective than it might otherwise have appeared.

Further, the creditor who lends to a married person has two avenues to collect: first against the borrower and, should the borrower be insolvent, next against her spouse. A creditor has a deeper well of insurance for claims against a married person than against a single one under the necessaries doctrine. Some states have modernized the necessaries doctrine by requiring that a creditor seek payment first from the spouse who actually acquired the debt. But other states allow action against either, allowing creditors to choose whichever spouse is easiest to collect from. Bankruptcy laws overlay the common law necessaries doctrine in structuring the management of spousal debt, but short of bankruptcy, the necessaries doctrine still operates.

The final place we see the duty of support operate in the ongoing marriage is when spouses attempt to contract around it. Many courts have denied spouses the ability to contract around their service obligation, by, for example, refusing to enforce a wage agreement exchanging housework or personal care for money if the parties to the agreement are married.[4] The contract is thought to be illusory, because these obligations are already owed to one another. This has had an impact in odd places, as, for example, when a court refused to recognize a wage contract between spouses that would have permitted one spouse to successfully claim paid labor under a prison work-release program.[5]

These three common law concepts — privacy or nonintervention, coverture, and the duty of support and services — influence much of the common law response to the ongoing marriage across different legal disciplines. In the modern era, there are also statutory responses to the ongoing marriage, discussed below.

Impact of Marriage on Property. While marriage changed the way property was managed and controlled, it did not change how property was owned at common law. That tradition continues in 41 states: Property owned by one spouse prior to a marriage belongs to that spouse during the marriage. Even property acquired during the marriage in these states is the separate property of one or the other spouse, unless spouses put both names on the title or otherwise indicate a gift or sharing of ownership. Sharing of property ownership does not happen by virtue of the marriage itself in the 41 common law states today.

Over the course of the second half of the nineteenth century, in response to a reform wave, states passed versions of Married Women's Property Acts, giving wives greater ability to control and convey their separate property. Even prior to the Married Women's Property Acts, some courts developed devices to mitigate the impact of a wife's complete loss of control over the future of her property. They would devise trusts, for example, that would allow her some greater control over her property and could prevent her husband's creditors from accessing it. The Married Women's Property Acts addressed the issue more systematically. Shortly after those acts were passed, earnings statutes gave women the ability to enter contracts exchanging their labor for wages.

In the eight original and one modern community property state, the rules have always been different: By virtue of the marriage itself, any new property that is acquired by either spouse through their labors belongs equally to both spouses. Ordinarily property that is inherited or was owned by one spouse prior to the marriage will remain separate property, although it can transmute into community property if it is commingled with community property in certain ways. The title to all property acquired by the labors of either spouse are owned half by each, on the theory that they both contribute, even if in different ways, to the acquisition of all property. The partnership theory of marriage, then, is fully realized in the community property concept.

The origins of community property reflect the civil law heritage, from Spain or France, of the particular states that use it, while all the rest of the states bring their law forward from the common law of England. Those community property states are Arizona, California, Idaho, Louisiana, Nevada, New Mexico, Texas, and Washington, and they have always been community property states, in keeping with the civil law. Wisconsin is the only common law state to switch to community property, and it did so in the modern era — in 1983 Wisconsin adopted a community property regime by statute.

As we will discuss in Chapter 4, at divorce, the difference between community property and separate property states is small. In the past several decades, states have developed "equitable distribution" laws that allow courts to redistribute property from the title holder to the non–title holder in a common law state at the time of divorce. That redistribution of title makes the difference between community property and common law states less significant post-divorce than it once was. The main conceptual difference now between the two kinds of states is the way property is owned during the ongoing marriage.

During an ongoing marriage, an individual in a separate property state may manage her separate property as she chooses. As long as that property remains separate, and she does not guarantee her spouse's debts, it remains safe from her spouse's creditors (unless it is the purchase of a necessity). About half of common law states retain the option of a unique method of holding real property for married couples, called tenancy by the entirety. Tenancy by the entirety is a form of joint tenancy, meaning that each title holder has an undivided share (50%) while each is alive and a right of survivorship (a right to the whole property) at the other's death. Critically, though, with tenancies by the entirety, one party cannot unilaterally destroy the joint tenancy by selling the property. The property can only be sold if both parties agree. Some states that respect tenancies by the entirety have modified them somewhat to give a spouse some unilateral authority to mortgage the property. Other states don't allow the spouse to unilaterally mortgage any part of the joint property, and still others limit the amount that a spouse can unilaterally mortgage. This effectively creates a protected status for real estate held jointly by spouses in common law states. But other separate property, including bank accounts, has no such unique status and is for the most part treated as it would be for a single person.

A different set of issues attends the management of community property in an ongoing marriage. Traditionally, despite the joint ownership, husbands alone had the right to manage and control community property, significantly diminishing the difference between community property and separate property during an ongoing marriage (the consequences at death, however, were still real). In the era of sex equality, the community property states have crafted different solutions to the problem of management rights over community property.

Theoretically, both spouses are entitled to manage community property. Some states allocate management to both and require joint action on real property; others allocate management to both and both may act unilaterally; others allocate management to the spouse whose funds purchased the community property, and still others allocate control to the person whose name is on the property, such as a bank account or piece of real estate, even when both spouses have a community property interest in the item. Control over ownership of pensions, which are presumptively community property as well, is fertile ground for conflict, because the employer deals directly with the employee, who makes elections (e.g., for an annuity or lump-sum payment) that will affect that employee's spouse. In the absence of applicable pension-regulating statutes, which can require notice to spouses of adverse action on pension management, courts have upheld the right of the employee spouse to manage her pension unilaterally, assuming she does not make a gift of the property to someone outside of the marriage. Thus, in most community property states, as in common law states, the person who earns the money and titles it in his or her name retains practical control over it.

4. Modern Regulatory Approach to the Ongoing Marriage

For many private institutions, marriage serves as an administrative organization tool. Employers privilege marriage in the distribution of employee benefits such as health care or discounts. That organizational function of marriage by private actors can be highly consequential, and for some married people, it is the benefits bestowed by private institutions, rather than government, that make the ongoing marriage such an important status. Particularly in light of the high cost of private health insurance, one of the most significant aspects of being married may have little to do with state action.

Government also uses marriage as an organizing principle, and the consequences for an ongoing marriage may also be highly consequential. The statutory responses to marriage are too numerous to catalog here and run into the thousands. But we can highlight just a few to get a sense of the reach of law in the ongoing marriage.

A spouse who was never in the paid labor force nonetheless receives benefits from the Social Security system by virtue of a ten-year marriage to someone who has. This is the payment of a significant sum of money, out of the common payroll tax, that is given to spouses who have not paid into that system, by virtue of marriage. It is not a splitting of the wage-earners share but the offering of an additional share by the state on the basis of being married.

Spouses are taxed differently at the state and federal level during their marriage than they would be were they two single people. This has sometimes provided a benefit to spouses, especially where one receives no income from the paid labor market; but it is more often a burden, sometimes termed the "marriage penalty." Congress has addressed the marriage penalty in recent years, but different treatment of couples filing jointly versus individuals filing alone has been preserved.

A final example is another public law response to family dependencies, in the form of the Family and Medical Leave Act of 1993. Under that act, a person may take 12 weeks of unpaid leave from work without fear of losing her job to take care of a partner so long as they are married. Being a legal spouse under the FMLA obligates third-party private actors — employers — to provide protections in light of the marriage. This is only the slimmest sample of the countless statutes and regulations that influence the ongoing marriage and give it consequences. They are not ordinarily regarded as *family law*, but they are at least as significant as traditional domestic relations law to the experience of being a legally married person in the United States.

B. ONGOING FAMILY: THE PARENT-CHILD RELATIONSHIP

1. Parental Rights

An "intact" family, meaning two married parents living with their children, enjoy a well-respected freedom to make decisions about the welfare of their children and the appropriate way to raise them. The tradition has very old roots in U.S. and English common law, from a time when our conception of children and childhood was entirely different than it is today. Today we view children as vulnerable, in need of and entitled to nurturing, protection, housing, food, and education. But in earlier times they were viewed as naturally inclined to evil, in need of correction and discipline, and supported by their parents in part so that their parents could extract labor from them. The roots of the parental prerogative were similar to those in master-servant law: Parents could make optimal decisions about how many resources to invest in a child in light of the expected labor return.

Today's continuation of the deference to parents rests on very different rationales. Since the early twentieth century, the Supreme Court has made clear that parents are entitled to deference in their parental decision-making because that deference serves both the polity's need for a heterogeneous citizenry and adults' need (or strong desire) for freedom to rear their children as they choose. The first rationale suggests that the Constitution protects parental liberty not so much because that liberty is good for parents but because key aspects of individualistic American culture will be undermined if the state asserts too much control over how children are to be raised. The second rationale has been explained as a personal right, analogous to a variety of other constitutive and expressive freedoms (speech and religion, for instance). Affording parents the right to bring up their children as they choose is thought crucial to human flourishing because rearing, teaching, and loving one's children, though a tremendous amount of work, can be such a defining part of who one is. Moreover, it may be impossible to do any one of those jobs — rear, teach, or love — without doing the others, so if one is thought crucial to human flourishing, the others have to be included in some concept of parental rights. The fact that most international human rights charters now include a right to parent indicates that the United States is not alone in its allegiance to parental rights.[6]

Doctrinally, the Supreme Court has suggested that parental rights are privacy rights, included in the "private realm of family life which the state cannot enter."[7] Privacy may not be the most accurate way of describing what the Court feels bound to protect, though. The cases suggest that parental autonomy is what matters to the Court. Thus, some parents have been granted the right to withdraw their children from public school to raise their children in a desired religious community even if in so doing they eschew state mandatory education laws.[8] Married parents are also entitled to a presumption that they act in their children's best interest.[9] In other words, in the first instance, the state must defer to parental decision making. Although some commentators have criticized the parental autonomy doctrine as insufficiently protective of children's interests, as recently as 1989, Justice Brennan, a liberal icon on the Court, wrote that "I think I am safe in saying that no one doubts the wisdom or validity [of the parental rights cases]."[10]

It is easy to assert, as the doctrine just discussed does, that parents know better than the state what is best for their children. Would it matter if there were evidence to the contrary? That parents know best for their children is not accepted because it is a provable, empirical point, but as a philosophy. For it to be true, it must be the case that there is not one, or even just a few, best ways to raise children, but many best or right ways, all of which are superior to what a state could produce with interference and undercutting of parental authority. We do not actually know that parents know best; we just believe that they do. If the law applies that belief consistently, it must accept a variety of different approaches to parenting.

Because of the apparent consensus on the importance of parental decision making, it may be a surprise how limited parental prerogative and autonomy are. Two parents are entitled to a presumption that they act in their child's best interest only if they agree with each other. If they are divorced or never married and they find themselves disagreeing with each other over how best to raise their children, neither parent is entitled to a presumption. Their competing entitlements to deference cancel each other out. In this regard, divorce impairs parental rights. We discuss how extensive this impairment is in Chapter 4.C. Just as important, child welfare statutes, initially passed at around the same time the Supreme Court articulated the parental autonomy doctrine, have come to undermine the notion of deference to parents, most often when those parents lack resources. We turn to child welfare statutes next.

2. Child Protective Services

A movement to protect children who were destitute, hungry, or abused began in the late nineteenth century. Today, every state has a statute designed to protect children from harm that gives the state the power to override parental authority in a number of ways. In addition, federal statutes using the spending power set out certain requirements for the operation of those state statutes. Behind parental prerogative and privacy to manage children as parents see fit is a reality of children both physically abused, sometimes to the point of being killed, and children whose basic needs are so neglected as to endanger them. States must decide how to protect at-risk, abused, and neglected children while respecting the superior role of parents in judging children's needs.

One way to reconcile this tension is to have the mechanism for a state to protect children be benign. Theoretically the state can provide children and parents with the support that they need while living together to reduce the risk of abuse or neglect by parents. Rather than assume that children are at risk due to unredeemable and venal parents, child welfare statutes can respect parental rights by providing resources that have been demonstrated to reduce the likelihood of abuse or neglect. Examples include housing assistance, drug treatment, parenting classes, childcare, medical or legal assistance, and counseling. Child welfare agencies can provide basic social work to connect people in need with available resources, thereby reducing the risk to children living in households where danger is a product of limited resources or skills. This aspect of the child welfare system posits the state as a support system to families under stress.

Sometimes these measures don't work, however, or the danger is so grave that there is no time to test them. In those cases, all states authorize state actors to step in between parent and child and remove children from their homes. This is the side of child welfare law that is not aimed at supporting parents and families as a unit but at protecting a child at all cost. Most people think the state should do this when a child is in danger. The critical and controversial question is what counts as danger. It cannot be adequate cause to remove a child from a family that a better or safer family can be found: If half of families were below average in the safety they provide to children, and therefore those families were at risk of having their children removed, the state's authority would be tyrannical. So the child welfare mission is twofold: Protect and support children within their families to the greatest extent possible, but remove children when they are in grave danger.

Social welfare agencies and courts are charged with applying that basic standard. Each state has created an agency to manage its child welfare program. Typically called the Department of Social Services (DSS), these agencies are given a range of tools with which to protect and support children at risk of some kind of harm. An awkward tension accompanies their mission, because the same agency, the very same social worker, has the ability to provide families with services that will improve the welfare of its children and at the same time the ability to proceed to remove children from their parents temporarily or permanently. Social service agencies typically approach a family offering services, but the same families justifiably fear the ultimate power of the state over their household.

In recognition of this difficult balance, state statutes create standards that must be met before a child may come under the jurisdiction of the child welfare agency in any way. Unwelcome "supportive" intervention cannot be pursued at random, but only after a determination that a child is at risk. Because jurisdiction over a family or child, even for supportive services, imposes intrusions on the family's privacy in the form of visits and evaluations, conversations, meetings, and recommended remedies of a discretionary or mandatory nature, that jurisdiction cannot be based on social judgments about poverty or difference unless they are tied directly to danger to a child. But the value placed on child protection leads to a system that is over-inclusive in identifying at-risk children. Typically, state statutes mandate that a child must be labeled "in need of services" for child welfare agencies to gain jurisdiction over that child and thereby insist on the provision of services.

Statutes define "in need of services" in a range of ways — some specific, some more general. A typical statute would allow for jurisdiction when a child is without food, clothing, shelter, education, or other required care because of parental inability or unwillingness to provide or is abused physically or emotionally or resides with someone else who is abused physically. Federal law[11] mandates the minimum form a state's definition of abuse must take. Child abuse or neglect is any recent act or failure to act (1) resulting in imminent risk of serious harm, death, serious physical or emotional harm, sexual abuse, or exploitation (2) of a child, (3) by a parent or caretaker who is responsible for the child's welfare. The federal government also mandates the minimum definition for sexual abuse. The federal statute does not prevent states from defining abuse or neglect or sexual abuse more protectively, but it must include the standard set out in federal law.

We have to distinguish between jurisdiction over a family — to intervene in any way — and the nature of the actual intervention. Being labeled a "child in need of services" under a statute may lead to nothing more than periodic visits from a social worker and conversations about health and safety. The above list is not what leads to the removal of a child from a family, necessarily. It is a list of circumstances that, if proven, may force upon a family state intervention of a range of varieties, against the family's wishes. For jurisdiction over a family to provide services, one of these risks must be shown in a court.

All statutes give social welfare agencies the authority to intervene in families on an emergency basis to prevent imminent harm, by, for example, removing children from a dangerous home. Even then, the agency must go into a court to make an evidentiary showing justifying jurisdiction within a short period of time, usually two or three days. The agency must then go again to court within a week or two, this time allowing the parents to appear and refute facts or judgments presented by the agency. Parents may fight either the assertion of any jurisdiction over the family or the particular actions taken by an agency, conceding the legitimacy of jurisdiction.

That may sound like solid process. But for many families over whom jurisdiction is sought, the resources or know-how to fight a finding that a child is "in need of services" aren't there. The majority of proceedings are brought for neglect, not abuse. The difference is that neglect is often a reflection of resources. For example, children are "neglected" when they are left at home at primary-grade ages because there is no adult to take care of them. That is more likely in a family where everyone works and there are no additional dollars to provide for child care. Similarly, some neglect proceedings surround hygiene — dirty or overcrowded living quarters, for example. Those are also sometimes a reflection of resources. When the state seeks jurisdiction over such a child, it is unlikely that the opportunity to appear in court and make a good argument against jurisdiction can be effectively used by parents stretched that thin. There is no constitutional requirement that a lawyer be provided to such a family, and most states do not provide one. Thus, the opportunity to appear in court to fight agency jurisdiction is unlikely to be meaningfully used, and jurisdiction sought will be jurisdiction granted.

Periodically, we see newspaper accounts of children who are killed or horrifically abused while under the jurisdiction of child welfare agencies. This scenario happens not because the social welfare agency failed to assign a social worker who would visit and monitor the at-risk children and prescribe parenting classes or impose requirements like drug treatment on parents. It happens because the actions taken, once jurisdiction was accomplished, did not prevent the escalation of abuse, and the agency made the wrong judgment about whether the danger in the home had become so grave that the child should be removed. These are horrible occurrences. In legal terms, it is important to understand that they are usually failures in the disposition — the action taken — not in the proper identification of a child in need of services. It is also important to understand that more aggressive agency action could easily run afoul of the constitutional rights of parents, although the parents may lack the wherewithal to assert their rights.

Mandatory Reporting.   The primary way children are identified as needing services is by being a sibling of a child already identified as in need of services or otherwise sharing a home with a child similarly identified. But for the initial foray into a household or family, abuse and neglect are ordinarily detected by the state because someone has made a report of suspicion as to a child's safety. All states have mandatory reporting laws that require some enumerated set of people who interact with children, such as physicians and other health-care providers, teachers, child-care workers, other educators, and public safety employees, to report a family to the department of social services if they have "reason to believe" that a child is endangered. Some states require "all persons" to report to the state reasonable suspicion of child abuse.

Failure of a "mandatory reporter" to report abuse to a law enforcement agent or social welfare agency can lead to misdemeanor-level criminal charges, or civil liability, depending on the state. The federal government conditions federal funding for child abuse prevention on states having a mandatory reporting system. The Child Abuse Prevention and Treatment Act[12] (CAPTA) was first passed in 1974 and has been reauthorized and amended several times since then. It requires states to extend immunity to those who report child abuse "in good faith." It is therefore a greater legal risk to fail to report suspected abuse than it is to report it with only a suspicion.

Family Preservation Versus Permanency Planning.
The pendulum in child welfare law swings over time between

two goals sometimes in tension for children in need of services. On the one hand, a high priority is placed on family preservation, meaning keeping a child in her home or returning a child who has been removed to her home as soon as needed improvements have been made in the home to ensure the child's safety. This goal reflects the constitutional and common law doctrine and belief that children are cared for best by their parents. On the other hand, children who have been removed from a home and placed in foster care are in limbo while state agencies work to ready a family for their return. They may not return to their old homes, but they are not available for permanent adoption into new families, either, because efforts are being made to return them to their families. What results from this tension is sometimes termed "foster care drift": Children stay in foster care, sometimes for years, waiting for a final disposition. In some cases, they move from one foster home to the next. The majority of foster families endeavor to provide well for their charges, but in many cases the foster care situation is not safer emotionally or sometimes physically than the original home. For these children, the child welfare agency has intervened on their behalf, disrupted relationships with the original family, only to provide a temporary situation not much superior to the original, and one that by definition is without a stable future, because foster families know that they are a temporary stop in a child's life. Permanency planning, which means working toward terminating parental rights so that a child may be adopted by a new family, is a principle that pushes back on the goal of family reunification in many cases.

In 1980, the federal government weighed in on behalf of family preservation, enacting the Adoption Assistance and Child Welfare Act (AACWA). AACWA focused on child abuse prevention and family reunification. It required states to make "reasonable efforts" to prevent the need to remove children from their homes and to facilitate children's return to their homes as soon as possible. Once a child was in foster care,

AACWA mandated that a case file and plan be created focused on reunification. Those files were to be reviewed by courts and agencies every 6 months, with a "dispositional hearing" after 18 months. At that hearing, if the state failed to demonstrate its reasonable efforts to reunite the family, termination of parental rights would not be granted. Under AACWA, many in the social welfare field believed that foster care drift worsened as social workers endeavored to repair families that were beyond repair.

In response to perceived failures associated with AACWA and foster care drift, the federal government tacked back toward permanency planning in 1997, with passage of the Adoption and Safe Families Act[13] (ASFA). ASFA removes the reasonable efforts requirement where there are aggravated circumstances, such as torture, abandonment, or sexual abuse, or where a parent has tried to kill or has killed another child, or where the state has terminated the parents' rights with respect to a different child. Under AFSA, a state is *required* to file a termination of parental rights petition if a child is in foster care 15 of the last 22 months, because the statute raises a presumption of parental unfitness in those cases. ASFA allows three exceptions: when a relative is caring for the child (called kinship care), when the state agency believes termination is not in the best interest of the child, and when a state agency has failed to provide the family with reunification services. Unlike the 18 months for permanency hearings under AACWA, under ASFA a permanency hearing must be held after 12 months. ASFA's presumption of parental unfitness after a child has spent 15 of his or her last 22 months in foster care has not been uniformly well received in state courts, which have challenged its constitutionality. The seesaw in priorities between AACWA and AFSA reflects the tension between the twin goals of reunification and permanency. In the end, parental rights termination, discussed in Chapter 4, can be the outcome of a child welfare intervention.

C. ONGOING FAMILY REVISITED

A strong tradition gives deference to ongoing families in decision making and protects them from state intervention. This deference is paid primarily to families with married parents, whose privacy for their relationship and for their child rearing is generally respected. In the absence of a marriage, parents are more vulnerable to intervention by the state at the urging of the other parent, as well as intervention by the state through the child welfare system. That system does have jurisdiction in married families as well but exercises it there rarely.

Alongside nonintervention as a family law principle, thousands of statutes and regulations respond to the fact that a couple is married, classifying individuals for the purpose of benefits or obligations. This latter category of statute is not often viewed as family law, but it provides one of the most significant consequences of family law's organizing institution: marriage. The apparatus of the administrative state responds readily to marital status.

The nonintervention impulse is viewed by some as a natural consequence of the unity of two individuals that marriage creates. By others, it is viewed as judicial reticence or incompetence to evaluate and adjudicate many of the disputes that arise between family members, even though judges will adjudicate those disputes if the family dissolves. By still others, nonintervention is viewed as a fictional unity between two distinct individuals who should not lose state protection and vindication of their rights and interests as individuals based on their marriage.

AACWA, AFSA, and CAPTA all belie the nonintervention principle and the notion that family law is the province of the states, not the federal government. When Congress grows concerned enough about children's welfare, it mandates that states act to protect children in the way that Congress thinks best. This results in extensive state intervention, usually into the lives of low-income families.

ENDNOTES

1. 381 U.S. 479 (1965).
2. 410 U.S. 113 (1973).
3. 157 Neb. 226, 59 N.W.2d 336 (1953).
4. *Borelli v. Brusseau*, 12 Cal. App. 4th 647 (1993).
5. *State v. Bachmann*, 521 N.W.2d 886 (Minn. Ct. App. 1994).
6. *See* the International Covenant on Civil and Political Rights, 1966, Article 21 §2 ("The right of men and women . . . to found a family shall be recognized.") *http://www.ohchr.org/english/law/ccpr.htm;* Charter of Fundamental Rights of the European Union, Chaper II, Article 9 ("the right to . . . found a family shall be guaranteed . . .") *http://www.europarl.europa.eu/charter/pdf/ text_en.pdf*
7. *Prince v. Mass.*, 321 U.S. 158, 166 (1944).
8. *Wisconsin v. Yoder*, 406 U.S. 205 (1972).
9. *Parham v. J.R.* 442 U.S. 584, 602-03 (1979)
10. *Michael H. v. Gerald D.*, 491 U.S. 110, 143 (Brennan, J. dissenting).
11. Child Abuse Prevention and Treatment Act, 42 U.S.C. 5101, *et seq.* (Jan. 1996).
12. 42 U.S.C. 5101, *et seq.*
13. 1997 P.L. 105-89.

⌒ 4 ⌒

Family Dissolution and Reorganization

J ust as families may develop slowly through relationships but have one bright-line moment of recognition from the legal system, so too families grow up and grow apart in a number of ways. This chapter looks at how legal family ties are severed or reorganized. We will first discuss the process of family dissolution for married couples and then discuss how family dissolution affects children.

A. THE GROUNDS FOR DIVORCE

To understand the law of marital dissolution today, one needs to understand more about the legal treatment of marriage historically. As suggested in the introduction, for a long while secular and ecclesiastical authorities shared jurisdiction over marriage. In this country today, it is still the case that a marriage performed by someone with religious authority to do so is usually a valid marriage for state purposes. The deputization of religious figures is notable in a country that prides itself on the separation of church and state, but it is rarely questioned.

In the fifteenth and sixteenth centuries, secular parties began to be concerned about asserting influence over the institution of marriage, probably for the same reason the church had been: Governmental bodies want to make sure that they have some control over sexual activity and the reproduction that can result so that governments can ensure that children are cared for. Thus, marriage was used by both the church and the state to confine sexual activity to certain relationships (marriage), and both authorities declared that children of a marriage were to be provided for by husband and wife. As an economic matter, during this time, husband and wife also remained a productive unit, primarily responsible for producing what they consumed and not responsible for producing much more than they consumed. During this period, secular authorities did not appear interested in altering the other defining characteristics of marriage. Marriage remained a consensual union between one man and one woman; its primary purposes were for child rearing and for the orderly disposition of real property in the case of the wealthy, and it should last forever.

When marriages lasted forever, there was little need to worry about the financial or other consequences of separation. There was no divorce. As discussed above, if women were abandoned by their husbands they could petition, first to an ecclesiastical court and later to a secular court, for something called a *separation from bed and board*. This would entitle the wife to monetary payments from the husband and keep him from reentering the home, but it did not dissolve the marriage.

Most of the Protestant denominations that broke off from the Catholic Church during the Reformation rejected the indissolvability of marriage, however, and Judaism and Islam have always had provisions for divorce. The more widespread divorce became as a religious matter, the more the secular state had to accept it. To be sure, divorce was still rare in the seventeenth and eighteenth and even nineteenth centuries. What spread was a theory of why divorce might be appropriate, not a tendency to actually get divorced.

A theory of divorce is important in a regime in which marriage is not necessarily permanent. People began to view marriage as less inevitably permanent as marriage began to acquire new defining characteristics. By the eighteenth and nineteenth centuries, people had begun to view marriage less as a locus for economic production and more as a social unit for which companionship (sexual and otherwise) was critical. Reproduction had to be a part of the bargain, assuming relevant sexual conduct, because there was no adequate birth control. But people came to view spouses, and spouses came to view each other, less as business partners and more as friends. Once companionship became a part of the marital bargain, though, there needed to be a remedy if one spouse turned into a bad companion. Fault divorce provided a remedy. One party could exit the marriage if he or she could prove that the other party was at fault by failing to be a good companion. Allowing people to divorce also freed them to marry other companions.

In the early days of this country, in order to get a divorce based on fault, one had to petition a state legislature. Legislatures usually granted a divorce only if one of the parties had acted abominably or one spouse had significant political power with the legislature. What counted as abominable was gendered. Women might be able to get a divorce if they could show extreme physical and emotional abuse, at least intermittent desertion, and failure to adequately provide. Men might get a divorce by showing one act of infidelity on the wife's part.

By the nineteenth century, legislatures had abandoned the practice of deciding divorces on an individual basis. Instead, each legislature had codified, in statute, what would count as sufficient fault for a divorce issued by a court. The usual list included adultery, extreme cruelty, abandonment, insanity, and impotence. One party had to prove the existence of one of these grounds before a court would rule the parties divorced.

The other party could defend against divorce with a variety of other accusations, including collusion (both parties wanted a divorce and had acquiesced to the underlying fault), recrimination (both parties committed marital transgressions), and condonation (the innocent spouse had resumed marital activity — living and sleeping together — after knowing of the marital transgression).

These defenses reveal just how confused the law was about marital fault. Both collusion and recrimination construct the marriage itself as a kind of punishment. One is not entitled to the benefit of divorce if one has acted badly oneself. The benefit of divorce went only to an innocent party wronged by a guilty one. If both parties were demonstrably cruel to each other, neither deserved the benefit of divorce. The perverse result was an ongoing marriage because both spouses were incapable of living up to marital ideals. The absurdity of sustaining the remains of such a marriage contributed to the decline of fault grounds. Comparably, condonation suggests that divorce is necessary not because one party acted badly but because the other party is so offended by the bad acts. If a spouse can forgive, then there are no grounds for divorce. This created a disincentive for forgiveness and attempts at reconciliation, despite the fact that forgiveness would seem an essential ingredient to a human relationship that is supposed to last until death.

The theoretically troubled fault regime existed for most of the nineteenth and twentieth century in America. If its intended effect was to keep marriages together, it was not successful. The number of divorces in the United States rose steadily throughout the nineteenth century and continued to rise through most of the twentieth century. There is a popular myth that divorce did not become prevalent until state legislatures did away with fault divorce in the 1960s and 1970s, but, in fact, the divorce rate (as measured by the number of divorces per couple married each year) rose at a fairly constant slope from 1870 through the 1980s, when it leveled off. Divorces went down during the 1930s when people did not have the money to go to court. They went up sharply right after World War II when the divorces that had not been finalized during the Depression were finalized and men returned from World War II to marriages that had not been able to weather the distance. Divorces went down again during the 1950s but then began a steady climb to the early 1980s. There is a slight blip when the no-fault rules were passed in the late 1960s, but the historical record shows that no-fault laws were passed in acknowledgment of rising divorce rates and in an effort to improve the litigation surrounding divorce. Many people even argued that a well-executed no-fault regime would curb the divorce rate, not exacerbate it.

People got divorced in the fault regimes because they wanted to. If only one party wanted divorce, but that party wanted it badly enough, he or she could usually persuade the other spouse to go along. He may have persuaded her by paying her off ("I'll give you the house and the kids and money if you let me go"). She may have persuaded him by demanding nothing if he would let her go. More commonly, probably, either could convince the other that he or she was miserable or in love with someone else. We do not have particularly good records for whether husbands or wives were more likely to ask for divorce, but it does not appear to have been a gendered phenomenon. It is not easy for either a husband or a wife to share a home and a life with someone who really does not want to be there. Many married couples recognized this long before the law suggested that not wanting to be there — *irreconcilable difference* — was a valid reason for divorce.

To get the divorce they wanted, in the days of fault-only divorce, the parties often faked fault. One party made an allegation of extreme cruelty or adultery, and the other party went along. Both were determined enough to get out of the marriage that making a stretch of the truth in court may have seemed like an innocent formality. The parties knew they were lying; the lawyers knew they were lying; the judges knew they were lying. No one was willing to stop the process because no one was willing to force two people that really wanted to be divorced to stay together.

The modern no-fault divorce reform movement started in earnest in the mid-1960s. It attempted to stop blatant flaunting of the fault rules by eliminating the fault requirement. The reform effort was also fueled by a desire to curb the rising rate of divorce. The goal was to replace a focus on fault with a focus on couples therapy. Divorce would only be possible after the parties had seriously examined their marriage, preferably with a trained psychologist or social worker. If the parties were less interested in proving fault, they could more effectively examine whether their marriage could be saved, and if not, make its end less hostile. Fault rules encouraged the parties to focus on what was wrong. A better divorce process would encourage them to focus on what was right, so that they might salvage the marriage. No-fault divorce was supposed to take longer (there were mandatory waiting periods, often of up to two years) but be less contentious. The parties were supposed to use the time provided to make sure they understood the negative consequences of divorce and the potential benefits of staying together. Marriages could end if there were irreconcilable differences, and judges were supposed to determine whether the differences were irreconcilable.

The no-fault idea spread quickly. By 1975, virtually all states adopted some form of no-fault regime. A minority of states retain both fault and no-fault rules. If the filing party has provable fault against the other spouse, that party can opt for either no-fault or fault-based divorce. Fault rules usually render judgments more quickly, bypassing the waiting periods most states impose between filing for divorce and the final order. Fault grounds are sometimes used today in cases involving domestic violence. They are also used when a party wants a speedier divorce, ordinarily when one party has a desire to remarry quickly. In some states, a finding of fault gives a judge discretion to alter alimony payments to the detriment of the guilty party. This kind of alimony order is usually done when the fault is domestic violence or financial misconduct, such as spending family resources on a paramour, hiding assets, or making gifts of family resources to siblings or parents to keep them out of the marital estate.

To the extent that no-fault rules were designed to keep marriages together, they have not succeeded. No state was willing to finance the therapeutic process that was supposed to accompany the no-fault regime. Professional psychological help costs money, and many judges were suspicious of it. The trial court judges who had resisted serious evaluation of the fictive pleadings submitted to them in fault divorce pleadings also resisted serious examination of the quality of the marriages that the no-fault rules instructed them to evaluate. The judges were unwilling to tell two people who filed for divorce that they must stay together and wished to avoid the embarrassment to the court and the parties associated with parsing through the marriage details.

The waiting-period-as-time-for-reflection idea also failed in its execution. A variety of exceptions soon developed: If a couple had been in counseling, the time spent in counseling counted toward the waiting period; if they had been living separate and apart for a period of time, that time could count toward the waiting period as well. When a court was unwilling to apply an exception, the couples split up and waited. The wait was not particularly onerous because social norms with regard to nonmarital sex and cohabitation were changing rapidly; individuals could move on with their lives despite the waiting period for finalizing the divorce.

The number of divorces finalized within the first few years of the no-fault era suggest that the no-fault regime led to only a slight increase in the divorce rate. Moreover, given the socially tumultuous time during which the reforms were implemented, it is difficult to tease out whether the increase in the divorce rate was a response to the changed law or instead to changed norms. The period between 1965 and 1980 marked rapid transformation of cultural norms with regard to sexuality, gender roles, family, and conformity in general. It would be surprising if all of those transformations had no effect on the divorce rate independent of the introduction of no-fault grounds.

There is also some evidence that the increased divorce rate that accompanied the no-fault reforms was due more to sexual behavior in the 1950s than legal reforms of the 1960s and 1970s. The 1950s saw a significant increase in premarital sexual activity, much of it without adequate contraception. When an unmarried woman got pregnant, most couples got married. The number of white brides pregnant at the altar doubled during the 1950s and the rate of teen births was higher than it is now. It was this cohort of marriages that produced the spike in the divorce rate in the following decades. As contraception use has expanded and as middle- and upper-middle class women started going to college in much larger numbers, the age of first marriage has risen steadily and the divorce rate, particularly for college-educated couples, has declined. In any case, the divorce rate for all marriages had stabilized by the early 1980s. As measured by the number of people who get married and then actually get divorced (as compared to the incidence of marriage and divorce in any given year), the divorce rate has never risen above 40 percent. Most demographers are predicting that it will not rise in the future.

The no-fault regime did facilitate *unilateral divorce*, meaning divorce without an agreement between the spouses. Particularly in states without waiting periods or with numerous exceptions to waiting periods, no-fault rules made it possible for one party to demand divorce without reaching a mutual agreement. The spousal negotiation that characterized the "joint" decision to divorce in fault regimes was no longer necessary. Some scholars have argued that this left women worse off financially because they lost the bargaining chip that fault divorce had given them: They could no longer refuse to go along with the fault charade absent a favorable settlement. Empirical reviews of divorce settlements shed doubt on the extent of this effect. Despite the bargaining power that fault regimes seemed to give women, most women did not secure sizable alimony or property settlements at divorce. There may have been a psychological benefit to having to give one's permission for the divorce, but there does not appear to have been a substantial pecuniary benefit.

From some perspectives, then, the no-fault rules were completely ineffectual. They did not significantly alter the divorce rate or the kinds of settlements received, although they may have changed the framework for negotiation. But to the extent that reformers were concerned with bringing the law of divorce into accord with the reality of family life, they can be seen as more successful. As the recalcitrance of the trial court judges suggests, by the late twentieth century, few people thought that the law should keep two individuals married if those individuals really wanted to get divorced. People may have believed that married people should feel more compelled to stay married. But that conviction does not translate into a belief that the law should force people to stay together. It is one thing for the law to recognize an institution of marriage that, as a legal status, takes some time and effort and money to terminate. It is quite another to suggest that the law should block completely the efforts of two people who want to terminate the status and are willing to incur the costs of doing so. While most people then and now may agree that marriage should not be completely costless to exit, they also likely think that law should not be an impenetrable obstacle to exit.

Still, there are those who believe that the no-fault rules went too far. A few states have attempted to reintroduce fault rules in the form of *covenant marriage*. Covenant marriage is a voluntary choice made at the time of marriage licensing and requires fault before one party can exit the marriage. It was created legislatively in a movement aimed at reducing divorce. Yet, as passed, even this anti-divorce reform allows for bilateral no-fault, meaning no-fault agreed to by both spouses, if the couple will suffer a longer waiting period. Covenant marriage has not been around long enough for us to know whether any participants will feign the same stories that litigants of old did. It is possible they will not, because demographic evidence suggests that the people most likely to opt for covenant marriage are those least likely to get divorced under any regime. Among the characteristics that make a couple less likely to divorce in any circumstances are a strong religious orientation coupled with a belief that marriage is a religious commitment, a belief in traditional gender roles, and middle- and upper-middle-class status.

While the move to no-fault in some ways brought the law of divorce into accord with contemporary mores and abandoned a system that was internally confused, it generated a new source of confusion. The fault system, at its core, maintained the principle of marriage as permanent: The promise to marry was a promise to stay together forever, unless there was fault. This made it easier to understand what the process of property distribution at divorce was supposed to do — it continued marital obligations beyond the end of the marriage, to the forever point originally promised. Requiring the at-fault spouse to pay the ex-spouse made sense precisely because the at-fault spouse had done something wrong. Comparably, an at-fault spouse could not realistically request support after divorce because she was the one responsible for the demise of the marriage that was supposed to provide for her. But under the no-fault regimes, there is no blame. Thus no one seems automatically entitled to or barred from receiving support from the other spouse postdivorce. That left the no-fault reformers with the question of whether, if neither party is at fault, either party is entitled to any kind of property or payment. If "forever" is no longer part of the bargain, what responsibilities should the parties have toward each other after divorce?

The initial answers seemed to be little or none. The prominence of the women's movement in the 1960s and 1970s aided the no-fault reform movement's ability to answer those questions in the negative. Because women's increasing labor force participation and legal equality suggested to some that ex-wives would be able to take care of themselves, the law became less willing to tie people together with postdivorce obligations. The new ideal that emerged in the no-fault era was one of parties going their separate ways entirely at divorce.

The next chapter examines the ramifications of that thinking in more detail, but the foregoing foreshadows some of the problems with that ideal. Assumptions about the achievability or desirability of post-marital independence and autonomy exist in some tension with the premise of marriage. If the law is going to treat the parties at divorce as fully independent individuals, primarily responsible for their own welfare and their choices, what purpose does marriage serve? Marriage is not, as it was many years ago, the economy's basic site of production. Although reproduction is still a part of most marriages, it is a much less essential part given birth control and a much less extensive part given greater life expectancy. Companionship still defines how most people view marriage, but without obligations, how is marriage different than friendship? Why treat husband and wife differently than friends or business partners? Most marriages do not look like most friendships or most business deals. There tends to be more emotional and financial interdependence between spouses than between friends. There tends to be more trust and less explicit contracting between spouses than between business partners. There also seems to be a consistent, if not universal, tendency for marital roles to develop, usually in ways that track gender.

Women's equality may allow women to achieve whatever men can achieve professionally. But married women are very likely to achieve less than their husbands professionally, for reasons often related to marital roles accepted by both parties. Any legal response will reflect some view about those marital roles. Should the law make different assumptions about the autonomy and independence of married persons than it does about single ones? Is it marriage, or instead gender, that tends to make people dependent on others, and is that dependence something to recognize and support or to ignore and discourage? The law assumes that parties share in marriage in a way they do not in business. Should the law force them to share? It appears that women systematically opt for less remunerative courses while married. Should the law respond to the gender aspect of that decision in any way or instead treat them as ungendered individuals who might as easily reverse their roles, even though they rarely do? The next chapter unpacks the ways in which contemporary family law attempts to address these questions.

B. FINANCIAL RAMIFICATIONS OF DISSOLVING THE MARITAL UNIT

With the advent of no-fault divorce, the typical family lawyer dedicates her time to questions of distributing assets when the marriage is over, not to questions of how to end the marriage. Nuclear families usually share most of what they have. The state must determine how to distribute what was once shared. The more a family has, the more decisions must be made. At divorce, there is sometimes property—a house, car, bank account, or pension — that must be divided, and there is future income that may be divisible. Questions arise over whether to characterize a given asset as property or future income. In addition, there may be questions regarding children's share of the marital wealth and questions regarding how to allocate parental rights and responsibilities.

While the typical family lawyer routinely deals with all of these issues, the typical divorcing family does not. In most states, the median net value of marital assets is approximately $25,000. There is often substantial marital debt to be divided, too. Most divorced women receive neither a property settlement nor alimony (also called maintenance). For most divorcing families, there are not enough assets to make a fight worth anyone's energy. This is another example of the class-based nature of family law. Just as state monitoring of child rearing is primarily applied to children in low-income families so the legal rules addressing finances at divorce are primarily applied to relatively wealthy people.

Divorced women are often quite poor. But the existence of so many poor divorced women does not necessarily indicate that divorce causes poverty. Many married couples are quite poor to begin with. When they get divorced, they get marginally poorer, but their poverty predates their divorce status. Living apart is more costly than living together. As one judge famously put it, one table cloth cannot cover two tables. Neither of those facts — that many women are poor to start with and that living apart is more expensive than living together — can be remedied by divorce *law*. What divorce law may be able to do is to allocate the burdens of divorce fairly.

On average, divorced men are not as poor as divorced women. This may mean that the law does not allocate the burdens of separation appropriately. But the disparity in wealth at divorce may also represent both cultural acceptance of gendered work patterns and cultural ambivalence about whether marital duties should survive divorce.

Divorced women who have left the workforce for some period of time or cut back on work hours are often not in a position to earn what their ex-husbands earn. Some may have chosen less remunerative but more flexible jobs that allowed them to take care of the family. Others wanted to leave competitive fields and gave up career-path time that they cannot get back because people who did not take time off are further up the ladder and the women further down will never catch up.

There is no societal consensus on whether divorce law should compensate for the income disparities caused by these kind of work patterns. Belief in the importance of individual agency and autonomy lead some to support a clean break at divorce. This would mean little ongoing responsibility between ex-spouses and that women should be responsible for the financially detrimental choices that they made while married. Those who see less autonomous decision making want to maintain spousal obligations postdivorce because they view work patterns that emerged during a marriage as joint decisions that benefitted both spouses and for which both parties should assume responsibility. This latter view may be a different version of autonomy, one that asks men to follow through on the bargains and choices they made in depending on home support provided by the gendered wives' role. In practice in the courts, judges prefer the clean-break view for shorter term marriages, especially if there are no children, and a more interdependent and collective view in longer term marriages and marriages where children led to more rapid role differentiation. This suggests that the pitched ideological battles may turn out to hinge on different versions of the facts of a divorce. We know that there are different kinds of divorces, and judges adjust their reactions depending on what kind of marriage is in front of them.

Section 1 below will start with the relatively simple explication of the ways in which divorce law divides the property of those who have enough of it. Section 1 will then go into the more complicated questions involved in determining what counts as property. Section 2 will analyze whether there should be anything to allocate after property has been divided. That is, to what extent is one spouse entitled to a share of the other spouse's postdivorce income stream (which is another way of describing alimony)?

1. Property Division

a. Title-based Jurisdictions

Historically, in most parts of the country, the common law practice required allocating property to its title holder at divorce. Married women were not allowed to control property before the Married Women's Property Acts passed in the late nineteenth and early twentieth century. This meant that men retained most property at divorce. Even after married women began controlling property, title-based jurisdictions still awarded the vast amount of property to men. This is because in the majority of states that followed the common law and not the community property tradition, men had the title to most property as a result of earning most of the money during the marriage. In a title-based jurisdiction, a woman could leave the marriage with property she owned at the outset, and she could retain anything that was titled in her name during the marriage. But most women were not earning money with which to purchase property in their own name during their marriages, so they were left with little property at divorce. For this reason, title-based jurisdictions often compensated with more generous alimony or support awards. Property is less contingent than alimony on behavior and on the ongoing solvency of the parties, so an alimony award is a consolation, not an adequate substitute for property.

b. Community Property Jurisdictions

As described in Chapter 3, eight American states have never followed the common law practice of assigning ownership of property within a marriage to the purchaser of it. Instead, those states adopted the practice of much of continental Europe, which treated all property owned by either spouse as jointly held, as long as it came from the efforts of either spouse during the marriage. In addition to the eight historic community property states, one state, Wisconsin, changed from common law to community property in 1983. Generally, inherited wealth was not shared in community property states; only property earned during the marriage was considered common. As in common law states, title controlled the distribution at divorce, but title was entirely different, and so the result at divorce was different. At dissolution, husband and wife split the community property equally, thus leaving women in community property regimes with substantially more property at divorce than the women in common law jurisdictions had.

c. Contemporary Practice

In the last 60 years there has been a gradual convergence of divorce results between community and title-based regimes, although it may be more accurate to say that community-property ideas have won the day. No state today adheres to the traditional common law, title-based distribution system at divorce. Instead, common law states have adopted an *equitable distribution* system, the goal of which is a fair distribution of property according to principles set out in a state statute.

Just as inherited wealth is not a part of the community in community property states, not all property is eligible for equitable distribution in common law states. The equitable distribution process applies to different pots of property, depending on the state. There are two basic models for deciding what property is available for distribution. In a minority of states, all property titled in either spouse's name, no matter how or when acquired, is subject to distribution. These are called *hotchpot* states, because all property is thrown into one hotchpot for division. In a majority of common law states, certain property defined by statute is considered *marital property*. Marital property is to be distributed equitably at divorce. Property acquired during the marriage, unless acquired by inheritance, is considered marital property, so it mimics the rules for what constitutes community property. Property acquired by inheritance or owned prior to the marriage is classified as *separate property*. The marital property is available for equitable distribution, but the court cannot touch separate property acquired before the marriage.

In a hotchpot state, while all property held by either spouse no matter how or when it was acquired is available for division, everything in the hotchpot will not necessarily be divided equally. Likewise, in marital property states, the exclusion of separate property does not mean that courts will ignore the impact of each party's separate property when deciding how to divide the marital property over which it has jurisdiction. A court in a hotchpot state may give great weight to the fact that certain property was inherited and assign most or all of it to the spouse who holds title to it. Comparably, in a marital property state, a court may take note of one spouse's vastly superior inherited separate property and compensate by assigning more of the marital property to the other spouse.

Each state has a statute that guides courts in making an equitable distribution at divorce. In theory, an equitable distribution is just that — equitable, fair, appropriate, just, but not necessarily equal.[1] The statutory factors can be sorted into two categories: Some allude to the *needs* of the parties, and others allude to the *contribution* of each party to the acquisition of the property in question. Contribution includes the contribution as a homemaker in most statutes, allowing room for a more complicated theory of property acquisition than wages and financial investments. A few states list no factors at all but simply instruct judges to use their discretion to divide property equitably.

In the early years of equitable distribution in common law states, few presumptions operated, unless the statute explicitly stated a starting point. Without such a presumption, some courts hewed to the title theory. They might look for justifications in the statute to depart from allocating property by title, but they believed that without good justification, title was the default. Some statutes encouraged this thinking by listing title to the property as one of the factors to be considered. Even with the list of factors to be considered, without baselines, starting points, or presumptions, equitable distribution statutes appeared to invite open-ended balancing inquiries, with little predictability.

Over time in almost every state, presumptions or starting points arose through practice and litigation, and the most common such presumption or starting point today is that a 50-50 divide of property is equitable. When this functions as a starting point, it means that the factors are to be applied to raise or lower the divide from 50-50. When it operates instead as a presumption, good justification needs to be offered to diverge from that allocation. These are usually judicially operating practices; while some equitable distribution statutes do contain presumptions, most do not. There is also significant interaction between the rule governing property available for distribution — hotchpot versus marital property — and the appropriate norm for dividing property. In marital property states, the 50-50 presumption or starting point rests easier than it does in hotchpot states, where a 50-50 presumption could operate to divide equally one party's vastly superior wealth acquired prior to the marriage or through inheritance.

The evolution of the equitable norms of an even split have been supported by decades of argument over how to justify that divide. Scholars and judges focus on increasingly complex theories of contribution to explain awarding property to the spouse who did not earn money in the market. Interpretations of the various models of marriage — as contractual promise, economic operation, or as partnership — were spun out by courts, lawyers, and academics. The more persuasive these theories, the more entitled the lesser-wage-earning spouse appears, and the less accurate it is to describe her as dependent.

It is important to underscore that the goal of equitable distribution is not necessarily equal distribution — it is fair or appropriate distribution. Conceptually, therefore, it is perfectly appropriate for one spouse to get less than 50 percent of the marital property. This is particularly true if he or she has more earning power or more access to property, such as a future inheritance, from elsewhere. Sometimes one spouse will receive more than 50 percent if he or she has unusual needs. The 50-50 presumption is soft, and some deviation from it is normal in the process of weighing the factors that make property division equitable. As in all areas of law, property distribution is ordinarily negotiated and settled, not brought to court. The strength of presumptions and expectations may make those negotiations easier, while wide discretion gives lawyers a less obvious starting point for bargaining. The practice of treating an even divide as equitable smooths divorce practice and encourages settlement in most middle-class divorce cases, but it may not address adequately the earning power disparity caused by common role division.

Judges and lawyers are now comfortable with the interpretations of contribution, entitlement, and need that lead to a 50-50 divide in the average case. But that operating rule can be strained in exceptional cases, including those where substantial wealth is at stake. Those divorce cases were best represented in recent years by the *Wendt v. Wendt*[2] case. In that case, the amount being divided was upward of $100 million. The household roles were "traditional." Some commentators found claims of contribution by a homemaker to the acquisition of $100 million difficult to explain. Others emphasized the partnership and promise notions of marriage in an attempt to justify an even divide. While the exact divide is undisclosed, reports suggest she received less than half of the marital property, but far more than the 10 percent her husband had proposed. Nine years after *Wendt*, in *Polsky v. Polsky*,[3] an Illinois court awarded a 35-year spouse $184 million in marital property, exactly half of the couple's cash and assets, all of which had been acquired after the marriage. The wife's attorney emphasized their true marital partnership, although the wife was not formally employed by her husband's companies. These high-wealth divorces draw attention to the theories used to split property. But in most cases, the amount of property is small enough that a 50-50 divide may be justified by multiple theories of contribution, and courts are not asked to tease out which one is in use.

Community property states have changed as well. Three community property states — California, Louisiana, and New Mexico — require an even 50-50 distribution of all community property. Those states do not consider property owned before the marriage community property, so that property remains with the spouse who has title to it. The other community property states use a less exact rule to split the property *and* a more expansive rule that allows a court to consider separately held property when making its division. Thus most community property states let courts consider the extent of noncommunity property wealth before deciding what would be an equitable distribution of the available community property. Just as in marital property states, courts at times award more than half of the community property to one spouse, to reflect the fact that the other spouse has more separate property or greater earning power.

In all states that use marital or community property, there are questions about how and when property switches from being separate to marital or community. A home that was purchased by one party before the marriage is usually retained by that person, especially in a short marriage. But a house can *transmute* into marital property under some circumstances. If the house were used by both parties consistently over the course of a 35-year marriage and the couple lived in it, invested in it, and relied on it together, many courts will label it marital property. Usually, the extent to which a piece of property is commingled between the parties determines whether it is treated as marital property. In addition, it is common for an individual to gift or transfer individually owned property into the marital pot, at which point it becomes subject to distribution.

In some divorces, the hard question is not how to distribute the property; it is the antecedent question of what counts as property. For most people of means, their most important form of capital is human capital: the training and ability to make money in the future. What makes a 45-year-old doctor or junior executive or lawyer wealthy is not past earnings; it is that he or she will likely continue to earn an increasingly substantial income for the next 20 years. Much of what he or she has earned up until age 45 may also be tied up in pension plans, stock options, or partnership shares and other forms of wealth that are not readily accessible.

Pensions or tax-deferred retirement funds are among the most valuable assets a couple owns. The marital home is usually the other large asset at divorce. Neither the home nor the pension is easily divisible, though, for different reasons. If there are children involved, the primary custodial parent often wants to maintain the family home. Selling the home and dividing the proceeds is not an attractive option for those who want to maintain stability for children by keeping them in the same house. Some states have statutory preferences for keeping the family home. A pension is also hard to split. Usually, there are significant tax consequences to liquidating a retirement account. Many pensions cannot be accessed until age 65. Thus, both pensions and houses are considered lumpy assets.

A common solution is to simply give one spouse, usually the custodial parent, the house and the other spouse the pension. But this can be dangerous. A custodial parent who retains the home often ends up paying for more home than she and her children need or can afford at their necessarily reduced standard of living. In return she often leaves herself little or no nest egg for retirement.

In addition, while the pension-for-house split seems to solve the lumpy asset problem, the simplicity of the split often puts too little pressure on the parties to get an accurate valuation of the pension. There is a wry adage among family lawyers that the value of the pension is always equal to the equity in the house. Given the cost of the financial experts hired to assess the actual value of the pension, it may be to both parties' advantage to accept the adage. But for couples who have borrowed heavily against their home or who have not built up much equity, it can seriously disadvantage the party who retains the home. At the same time, the one who receives the pension but cannot access it still needs new housing and may have no practical way to finance it with all his wealth in an inaccessible pension.

There are ways to divide a pension or retirement account, but they can be costly. Most pensions are subject to ERISA — the federal law designed to provide some measure of retirement protection to employees. ERISA severely restricts when, how, and to whom employers can pay out pension benefits. If, in dividing marital property, a court or couple opts to divide a pension, then a court must issue a qualified domestic relations order (QDRO). A QDRO is a judicial decree requiring the employer to use pension funds to pay someone other than the employee, such as an ex-spouse, at a given time in the future. QDROs take time to draft, and therefore money, but they can be particularly useful in a relatively lengthy marriage in which one spouse has no other retirement fund option.

Many sources of wealth are even more speculative than pensions, however. Stock options can be worth almost nothing at the time of divorce but a huge amount five years later. Employees of new companies are often paid in stock options and accept a modest salary because they may profit from the company's success later. If an employee is paid with stock options during the marriage, those options are marital property. But if the company is young, it is difficult to determine how much stock options may be worth decades into the future. Yet the couple may have been counting on the stock options as part of a retirement package. At this point we can see why financial experts have become a ubiquitous part of higher-end divorce litigation, notwithstanding the cost of hiring them. Valuation of the stock options, or pensions or retirement accounts, is essential to their equitable division.

Experts are also needed if there are commodifiable but intangible assets. These experts put a value on human capital. Marital dissolution law gives incentive for an expert to put a present value on a party's future income and to characterize that future income as property — for example, goodwill, a professional degree, or a de facto claim to renewable commissions or royalties. The law is clear that property should be distributed fairly between the parties, and property dissolution orders, unlike alimony, cannot be modified later. Thus, if one spouse wants to claim a right to the other's future earnings, the safest way to do it is to label that future income stream property. If a wife can successfully label as marital property a husband's business goodwill — the likelihood of maintaining a future customer or client base — then the wife is entitled to approximately half, provided a convincing expert can place a present value on that goodwill.

This premium on quantifying a future income stream as property subject to distribution reached its height in the 1980s as a result of the clean-break divorce reform movement of the 1970s. The goal for this movement was to encourage parties to go their separate ways at divorce. Alimony, which ties the parties together, was discouraged. The ideal was to make the parties whole enough through property distribution. Thus, the rules of property distribution had come full circle in many states. Traditionally, in common law jurisdictions, wives got no property at divorce because everything was titled in their husband's name. If they got anything, it was a right to ongoing support from an ex-husband in the form of an alimony award. The reform ideal was to give the dependent spouse no ongoing support but instead enough property to make ongoing support unnecessary.

It turned out, though, that it was difficult to give a spouse, particularly one who had been out of the workforce for some period of time or had worked only part-time, enough property to make ongoing support completely unnecessary. In part this was because courts resist labeling many forms of human capital "property." Only New York state treats professional degrees as property. Other states find professional degrees and other devices that let people earn substantial income too personal to be treated as property. Many states refuse to treat goodwill as property. Turning a professional degree or a client base into an asset, half of which the earning spouse owes his ex-spouse, binds the earning spouse to a course of professional conduct that he may not want to pursue.

An ability to make money, and a likelihood that one will make money, are very valuable. But they are not the same thing as having made the money already. Accounting principles allow the value of earning potential to be discounted because it has not been realized, and the earning party may not want to earn, even though he can. This is especially true if he has to share it. Perhaps aware that divorce can change peoples' priorities, or perhaps concerned that commodifying human capital is dehumanizing, courts do not stretch to label potential future income streams as property, despite pleas from dependent spouses. Without claims to those income streams as *property*, and without adequate earning power of their own, dependent spouses need alternative theories of entitlement to those income streams. Alimony remains the primary mechanism for sharing future income postdivorce.

Despite the stated goal of eliminating or strongly discouraging alimony in the 1970s, alimony never really went away in divorces among the upper middle class or wealthy. Courts were too uncomfortable with the financial predicament of many women who had no decent property claim to their ex-spouse's substantial future income stream. Almost everyone who has studied the subject agrees that alimony — also termed *spousal maintenance* or *compensatory payments* — should be awarded in many cases, although no single theory of alimony satisfies everyone's intuitions and sense of fairness. What follows is a description of various theories of alimony.

2. Alimony

At one time divorce was less common and alimony represented the never-ending support obligation undertaken at the time of the marriage. The decreasing permanence of marriage, the decreasing relevance of fault, and the increase in women's economic power all complicated the prior foundation of alimony. There are now a number of different theories of alimony. Each seems applicable to some cases but inapplicable to others or indeterminate in many situations. The new foundation is an increasingly complex set of premises about the dependencies and entitlements created during marriage. Scholars struggle with the inability to fully theorize alimony. But the practice of courts has progressed nonetheless to include elements of a number of justifications. Implementation is imperfect, but it is less troubled than the failure of consensus on the theory. Today there is statutory authority in all states to award alimony, although not every divorce includes an alimony award.

Until the 1970s, in most states alimony was explicitly gendered. Statutes authorized courts to order husbands to pay wives, but courts had no authority to order wives to pay husbands. Before the Married Women's Property Acts, in common law states women and children had to rely on alimony. Child support did not exist apart from alimony. The award was referred to as *support*. Because women had not been allowed to acquire property during the marriage, they ordinarily had no property. Women were entitled to support pursuant to the marital bargain. A husband was only responsible for paying his ex-wife if a court had determined that he was at fault for the divorce; if instead she was at fault she could not receive alimony. At-fault men were responsible for paying alimony because they had broken the marital agreement, a critical component of which was providing for a wife and children. The support obligation they undertook when they married was considered unending and was said to survive the divorce.

The no-fault era necessarily changed that original understanding of alimony, and emerging notions of women's equality necessitated changing the explicitly gendered nature of alimony as well. In 1979, the Supreme Court found gender-specific alimony statutes unconstitutional under the equal protection clause.[4] If a statute allows a judge to award any alimony, the judge must be allowed to award it to both ex-husbands and ex-wives. Now either spouse can make a claim on the other's future income stream.

But treating alimony as a nongendered legal entitlement ignores most of what makes alimony theoretically challenging. Arguably, no theory of alimony can be properly understood or analyzed without appreciation for how gender and gender roles function both in society and within families. Indeed, the struggle over a theory for alimony today maps onto the struggle between two perspectives on gender roles today. The first view is that law should recognize and compensate for gender roles as they exist. The second is that law should instead assume that gender roles do not exist, both because many people wish that they did not and because equality doctrine sometimes appears to require that law ignore gender roles.

There is no doubt that both men and women can become financially dependent on a spouse. But women are far, far more likely to do so than are men. Alimony could be structured to discourage this kind of dependence by providing little to a dependent ex-spouse at divorce. This approach assumes that wives would be influenced to remain financially independent by the prospect of receiving no alimony at divorce. Some proponents of equality favor this course of action.

Alternatively, alimony could reflect the high value couples seem to place on women's traditional contribution to the home. We are able to assume that couples do value women's traditional home contribution highly because they routinely sacrifice some or all of a woman's earnings so that she can devote more time to household work and management. Role differentiation occurs, on this theory, for the benefit of all individuals in the household. On this theory, she has earned alimony with her role-differentiated contributions.

Another alternative is for alimony to reflect the unity or promise theory of marriage. Under this approach, a spouse's entitlement is based on the original promise of sharing within the marital unity. Marriage is a union of equals, even if the equals contribute differently. Some proponents of equality favor the course of action that gives women a strong claim on postdivorce income on one or both of the contribution or promise theories.

Alimony could also exist as a quasi-compensatory entitlement that rewards women for some of the non-remunerative work they tend to do in the home. It would take into account the standard of living achieved during the marriage but also assume that divorced women will have substantial ongoing responsibility to care for themselves financially in the future. Under this scenario, alimony awards are available but limited. This description may best captures how alimony is usually awarded today.

Which behaviors or circumstances entitle a spouse to a share of her ex's future income stream? A number of justifications come to mind: She earned it because she supported him financially and with her household labor (contribution); she earned it because of the sacrifices she made for the family (foregone opportunities); she's entitled to it because he promised to share (status); it's only fair that she be given a chance to become independent (rehabilitation). Most alimony statutes allow judges to consider all of these ideas, among others. Judges are thus left with a great deal of discretion to determine which theory of alimony, if any, seems most appropriate in a given case. Each of the theories of alimony have limitations as well as strengths.

It is possible to think of the first three theories of alimony in contract remedy terms. Rewarding a spouse for the contributions she made to the home resembles restitution. Recognizing the opportunities she passed up for the sake of the family resembles a reliance remedy. Allowing her to share in his income because that is what he promised at the beginning resembles an expectation award.

Like almost all other contract/marriage analogies, one must be careful in carrying the damages analogy too far. Spouses, unlike most contracting parties, usually find themselves falling into certain roles without ever negotiating them explicitly. Spouses may not experience their relationship in contractual terms; the social norms surrounding marriage suggest it is more than a regular contract, and the state does not view the arrangement in purely contractual terms. Nonetheless, as an initial matter, one can see the similarities. Undoubtedly, spouses do negotiate informally over countless matters both of daily life and long-term decision making. Falling into certain roles resembles course-of-conduct behavior in commercial contracts, from which it is possible to identify general understandings reflected in actions as well as words.

As in many contractual situations, there are times in which the different kinds of remedies will seem more and less appropriate. Take restitution, for example. Awarding an ex-spouse for her contribution seems like a fairly noncontroversial idea. Consider a short-term marriage when one spouse has supported the couple for a period of time so that the other spouse might enhance his human capital by going to school, for instance, or when she has performed readily marketable work for her spouse's business venture by keeping books in a small business. In those cases, it is relatively easy for courts to order the benefited spouse to repay his ex for the value of her services. This payment may even be with interest. But it usually will not include the expected return on her investment: an ongoing share in the increased earning potential.

In numerous situations, however, there will be no contribution that is easy to measure. If both spouses worked throughout the marriage, and if her support of his endeavors is not readily captured in objective value, restitution can seem inadequate. Often, the most important marital contributions that spouses make are those for which we cannot readily find market values: love, emotional support, care of children, and household organization. These are things that one cannot purchase on the market in full equivalence, and therefore we have difficulty assessing their monetary value. But in many marriages, they are precisely what the financially dependent spouse disproportionately contributed. It is of real value, but how can we compensate for it?

Thinking about her contribution in terms of foregone opportunities is one way to find a value for her work. Most statutes instruct judges to consider that alimony should compensate a spouse for her career sacrifices and put her in the position she would have been in if not for these sacrifices. If the couple decided to forego her market wages, her household contribution can be assumed to be worth at least that much to the couple. Some support substantial alimony awards based on this idea that the *opportunity cost* for foregone wage labor must be the minimum, though not maximum, value of her contribution to the household, or the spouses would have chosen to have her in the paid labor force, where she would have been of greater value to them.

Again, in some marriages, a reliance-type award can make sense. For instance, if the parties agreed that she would delay getting a degree or a promotion until he was finished with school, sometimes she can receive as alimony the difference between what she is able to earn at divorce and what she would be able to earn had she not sacrificed for the family. The longer the marriage, though, the more speculative this foregone opportunity inquiry becomes. Asking a woman who left the workforce 15 years ago what she would be doing if she had not left the workforce can be an indeterminate exercise in creative thinking. A woman who willingly gave up partnership track after only a few years so that she could stay home with her children might well have opted against partner even if she had not had children. Would the woman with an MSW when she met her husband have completed a PhD if she had not met him? Or would she have married the other guy, the one who made more money . . . or the one who made less? Would that other marriage have lasted and in that way been more satisfying? Should the spouse not chosen count as a foregone opportunity for which the chosen spouse should compensate? The truth about her alternative path is unknowable, because time moves forward.

How roles were assumed may also seem relevant. For some couples the decision-making on wage labor force participation may not have been jointly made. It may even have been the source of marital conflict. What if he wanted her to keep earning wages and she wanted to stop, or vice versa? The theory of alimony focused on her contribution also takes no account of the paying spouse's wage. In those cases where her job prospects had originally been better than his, some will doubt whether he should be responsible for all of her foregone opportunity costs.

There is a further problem, too, with using foregone opportunities or contribution as a measure for alimony. Gendered work patterns mean that women are likely to be foregoing less than a comparably situated man would because women tend to be in less remunerative jobs or fields to start with. Whether women *choose* these jobs because they are forced there by gender norms and gender discrimination or whether they choose them because these jobs are sometimes more compatible with family obligations is debated among labor economists. Whatever the outcome of that debate, an inquiry about the job a woman might have had asks a question that assumes a market in which women earn less. Is it alimony's job, meaning the job of marriage, to compensate for the gendered workforce? Many people may think not, but marriages, particularly upper-middle-class marriages, may benefit from the way gender roles function in society. Because women may be steered by gender norms or gender discrimination into more flexible, less remunerative work, heterosexual couples often have an easier time making income-maximizing decisions. Once it is clear that a woman earns less than her husband, each time a career sacrifice is necessary for the family, it will make financial sense for the lesser earning spouse to make that sacrifice. It is easier for couples to make decisions if one choice makes more financial sense than the other. But the fact that the same person always makes the financial sacrifice means that the income differential between the spouses will likely continue to grow. This in turn exacerbates, or justifies, the need for alimony.

Contribution and foregone opportunity inquiries are both backward looking. They require judges to look back at what the dependent spouse did in order to determine what she is entitled to in the future. These difficult assessments may be minimized with an alimony entitlement providing an ex-spouse adequate payment to live at the standard of living, or the status, established during the marriage. This is backward looking but not dependent on the receiving spouse's actions or priorities. It parallels what the law nominally aspires to for children (child support is addressed in Section C.1. below). It reflects the common aphorism that an ex-spouse should be kept in "the style to which she had grown accustomed." It also suggests that the source of the entitlement comes not from contribution but from what the higher earning spouse promised by marrying and through marital conduct. The promise to marry is a promise to share equally forever. The law no longer makes people stay married forever, although it could make people share forever, or until death or remarriage. But forcing a spouse to share half will not keep the other spouse in the style to which she's grown accustomed unless there was a large unspent surplus during the marriage. Two apart is simply more expensive than two together — two tablecloths cannot cover one table. If she lives at the marital standard of living, he cannot, and vice versa. So what is each one entitled to, exactly? Is the recipient entitled to just less than the marital standard of living? A reasonable amount less? Since both parties cannot have the actual marital standard of living, this concept provides no measure that can be implemented.

Courts could require the parties to share future income equally, without either enjoying the marital standard. But forcing the parties to share income indefinitely seems antithetical to the legal reforms that allow the parties to separate. No-fault divorce allowed the parties to leave each other's company, but many also believe it should allow them to get on with separate lives. An alimony standard that ties the two together because that was the nature of their original promise undermines most modern understandings of divorce. Thus a pure status or sharing standard is rarely if ever decisive, but it is often a factor. This is in part because of the inadequacies of the compensatory (restitution and reliance) standards, discussed above, and in part because of the inherent limitations with the anticipatory (need and rehabilitation) strategies discussed below.

With the advent of no-fault divorce, some reformers advocated an alimony standard with the only goal of allowing the more dependent spouse to get back on her feet. Effective independence may require temporary, forward-looking relief aimed at helping an ex-spouse obtain a position from which she could achieve independence. Usually these theories were referred to as *need* or *rehabilitation* standards. But the difference between surviving and thriving independently can be substantial. Does survival mean poverty level, or twice that? Fifty percent of the marital income, or half of that? With the foregone opportunities inquiry, we saw the challenge of finding her nonmarital baseline, and the problem is repeated here. To measure rehabilitation, we need to know where she was before she lapsed into that state from which she needs rehabilitating. We must decide whether the woman who left the law firm after five years needs more or less than the woman who never went to law school. The brilliant BA may spend her married life as a potter—rehabilitation describes her needs poorly. If it is alimony's job to help a woman "get back on track," we must investigate in a backward-looking process what track she should be on. Alimony is probably incapable of truly getting her back on the track that she was on: Either it is too costly, or we do not know what that track would be. Instead, the rehabilitation standard must pick an appropriate track for her now. With poverty too low and the marital standard of living too high, courts once again have no guidance to choose a standard in between.

One controversial economic theory posits that women are more valuable when they are young because these are their reproductive years and because some men find younger women more attractive than older ones. This same theory posits that men are more valuable when they are older, because their incomes rise over their lifetime. A man who enjoys the woman's high-contribution years early in the marriage, then divorces her before she receives back his high-contribution years, receives his part of this deal and does not provide hers. The saying "I gave you the best years of my life" captures this stereotype.[5] This argument is sometimes offered for substantial alimony to a woman who is divorced in what appears to be such a traditional arrangement, on the theory that she will not be able to remarry or remarry "well," given that her youth is gone. This theory is undermined by the data showing that most divorces occur within the first seven years of marriage. Most divorced women remarry and thereby regain their marital standard of living. Also, we cannot assume that a woman's failure to remarry is always a disappointment. During marriage itself, the substantial psychological evidence suggests that men are happier than women. This may mean the net psychological costs of the divorce are higher for men. It may also mean that failure to remarry for some women is not a punishment in overall well-being, even if financial well-being is lower.

As is probably clear from the given examples, different theories fit better for some marriages than for others. The shorter the marriage, the more objective the spousal contribution, the more a restitution-type payment makes sense. The more obvious the foregone opportunity, and the more feasible it is to compensate for it in a way that seems appropriate, such as with tuition payments for the dependent spouse, the more courts will award a reliance-type remedy. Conveniently, in those types of marriages, the reliance remedy and the rehabilitation remedy often look very comparable. If courts can understand what she gave up, it is likely that courts can assess what she needs to rehabilitate herself; those two figures will likely be the same. But the longer the marriage and the more substantial the nonquanitifiable contributions, the more abstract it is to determine what a life on her own or with a different spouse would have been. In those cases courts are likely to award long-term alimony without tying it to a restitutionary measure. These awards acknowledge that in light of the investment she made in the marriage, she is entitled to a share of her ex-spouse's income stream long after the marriage has ended. What she is entitled to can vary greatly. Some courts order the payor spouse to send a percentage of monthly income that the judge labels reasonable. Other courts examine the marital standard of living with more precision and use it as a reference to establish what she is entitled to.

No alimony award lasts forever, though. Awards are ordinarily written for a period of months or years, with an end date in the order itself. Some states have presumptive formulas that allow for alimony for half the number of months that the marriage lasted, although the formulas may be modified on relevant facts. Many payors prefer to pay alimony as a lump sum, so as to avoid ongoing contact with their ex-spouse. Alimony can also be modified if there is a substantial change in circumstances for either the payor or the payee. Whether short or long term, it ordinarily terminates at the death of either ex-spouse or at the remarriage of the receiving party. In many states it also terminates if the receiving spouse starts cohabitating with another partner. What counts as cohabitating varies greatly from state to state.

The justification for terminating upon remarriage returns alimony to its basis in the support obligation. The new marriage puts a new party in the position of taking on that support obligation by law. While cohabitation may include the sharing of resources to some degree, that sharing is not pursuant to legal obligation and therefore is not enforceable. From the alimony recipient's perspective, then, cohabitation ends the alimony obligation of the former spouse without starting an obligation from anyone else.

Given the extensive new analysis justifying alimony in the no-fault era, one might expect that courts would reevaluate the automatic termination of alimony at remarriage or cohabitation. After all, if alimony represents a restitution- or reliance-type award for past sacrifice of the spouse, there is no reason the award should terminate until it is fully paid off. In a few states, courts have been willing to examine the rationale for the alimony when a payor petitions to terminate alimony due to the recipient's remarriage. If the rationale were to reimburse the recipient for money she'd invested in her ex-spouse's education, some states will allow the alimony order to survive the recipient's remarriage. Indeed, a few states no longer have a rule that remarriage automatically terminates alimony, although the payor may petition based on the change of circumstances and will often be able to make a good case for termination of payments.

The fact that an alimony order is not a stable, final order is another reason why parties often prefer to achieve their goals in the property distribution instead. A property distribution is final, and the parties can structure their post-divorce lives knowing that any entitlements flowing therefrom will not be subject to change.

3. Alternative Dispute Resolution and Nonjudicial Distribution

We have described the legal framework for distributing property and income at divorce. In most divorces, that framework provides the background principles that allow parties to settle. In over 90 percent of divorce cases, the parties never ask a judge to divide property or distribute income streams. They negotiate the division themselves and ask the judge to approve it. The legal rules provide the theories of entitlement that help parties understand what they can demand and what they can refuse to give in settlement. The more discretionary and ambiguous the legal standard, the less certain the parties are of their entitlements.

There are a number of reasons why so many divorces settle. First, litigation is expensive. Money paid to lawyers is money lost to the parties to distribute between them. Litigation is emotionally costly, as well. Emotions run high during divorce proceedings. A dispute resolution system like litigation, which puts a premium on undermining the other party's arguments, can exacerbate feelings of spite, anger, and distrust between the parties. If there are remaining financial ties or if there were children in the marriage, the parties are going to have ongoing contact after divorce. It is in everyone's interest to keep negative feelings to a minimum. Moreover, the parties have little motivation to set precedent. In some commercial contexts, repeat actors have an interest in resolving a legal issue for reliance the next time, but in the divorce context, the parties have no such incentive. Few litigants envision getting divorced again, and even if they did, the inquiries are too fact specific to connect from the first divorce to the second.

Most settlements are negotiated by parties and their lawyers before going to trial. In these situations, litigation is used as a threat to push parties to settle, more than it is used as a dispute resolution device. There are more formal alternative dispute resolution devices used in the divorce context as well. Mediation, for instance, has grown increasingly popular in the last 20 years. Initially, all divorce mediation was voluntary, meaning that both parties chose to mediate their dispute. Now, a majority of states either mandate or strongly encourage mediation.

Divorce mediations are conducted by impartial mediators, some of whom are lawyers, but some of whom are social workers or psychologists or clergy. They are tasked with helping the parties come to an agreement, not with enforcing the law or advocating for the parties. There are no procedural or evidentiary rules governing what can be discussed, so the parties have an opportunity to air grievances and express desires that would be suppressed in formal legal proceedings. The emphasis is supposed to be on agreeing, not winning. Parties can mediate their entire divorce or just certain issues within it. Several empirical studies suggest that mediation leaves divorcing parties more satisfied with the process, less angry at their ex-spouse, more content with the financial settlement, and more willing to negotiate in the future than does traditional litigation-oriented negotiation.

Mediation is not without its critics. One of the most common criticisms surrounds cases involving domestic violence. To ask an abused spouse to sit down with her abuser and peacefully mediate a divorce settlement is unfair at best and traumatizing at worst. If a history of physical violence shaped the power dynamic between the parties, it is distressingly likely that the abused spouse will care too little about her financial entitlements and too much about appeasing her abuser. For this reason, most commentators recommend against mediation in cases of domestic violence.

The problematic dynamic inherent in domestic violence cases may be present in other cases as well. Because the law plays such a reduced role in mediation, we don't know whether mediation adequately protects those whom the law is designed to protect. For instance, parties report being more satisfied with mediated settlements, but that could be because bypassing pre-litigation strategy left them ignorant of theories of entitlement that might have benefited them. Mediated property awards and child support awards are comparable to those achieved through other forms of settlement, which is encouraging. But child support awards follow a formula, and property awards usually follow a 50-50 divide. Given the clarity of the background legal rules in those two areas, it is not particularly surprising that parties arrive at the same results regardless of dispute resolution forum. Both are more formulaic than alimony awards. The evidence comparing mediated alimony to other alimony settlements is less clearly favorable. This may reflect the fact that the parties are less likely to understand their rights to alimony. It is in the murkier areas, where entitlements are less clear, that mediation may be a problem for the less empowered party.

There are two other forms of alternative dispute resolution, one old and one very new, that are growing more popular in the divorce context. The traditional alternative to litigation, arbitration, is now commonly used in divorce—though not as commonly used as mediation. Arbitration is like mediation in that it enlists a nonjudicial, neutral third-party arbitrator to help resolve the dispute. But as in litigation, the parties are represented by counsel and the arbitrator, not the parties, determine the final outcome. The arbitrator's decision is submitted to the judge for final approval. If the parties voluntarily agreed to arbitrate, judicial review of the arbitral decision is limited to arbitrator misconduct or flagrant disregard of the law — unless there are children involved. Because of the state's *parens patraie* interest in children, many courts subject even voluntarily arbitrated decisions about children to special scrutiny.

As with mediation, parties can agree to arbitrate everything or just those issues that they cannot negotiate on their own. As also with mediation, some jurisdictions now require the parties to arbitrate before proceeding with litigation. Mandatory arbitration, like mandatory mediation, is not binding. Parties have the right to proceed to litigate if they want to bear the costs — and wait for a result. Alternative dispute-resolution procedures not only save money, they save time, with final outcomes reached in a fraction of the time a traditional legal proceeding would take.

The most recent dispute resolution idea is called *collaborative divorce*. It proceeds much like standard pretrial negotiation, with each party being represented by a lawyer who can advocate vigorously for his or her client. But with collaborative divorce, both lawyers disqualify themselves from proceeding with future litigation. The attorneys are hired to negotiate — and only negotiate. This means that the attorneys have no incentive to stonewall negotiations into litigation, and neither do their clients. The traditional threat to litigate is an empty one because the cost of hiring a new attorney is, for most clients, prohibitive.

Some argue that collaborative divorce presents the best of both worlds. Unlike mediation, clients are supported, educated, and protected by their attorneys, but the sole purpose of the proceedings is agreement. Critics of collaborative divorce argue that clients can feel undue pressure to come to an agreement. Also, a litigant who is comfortable and pleased with his attorney should, arguably, not be forced to change lawyers before pursuing his right to litigate.

Given the unrelentingly adversarial nature of litigation, it is understandable that alternative dispute-resolution proceedings have grown so popular in the divorce context. After all, the parties involved once did profess to love each other. There is nothing in the traditional litigation paradigm that encourages them to hold on to respect for that love. To the extent that alternative dispute resolution allows parties to emerge from divorce proceedings feeling better about themselves and the person they once decided to marry, they should be applauded.

The growing popularity of alternative procedures also suggests decreasing state regulation of marriage. Alternatives to litigation became possible as it became unnecessary for courts to determine fault. But the alternatives have grown so much that law's role in defining entitlements is on the decline. Particularly with mediation, where lawyers are usually not present, the law can be reduced to peripheral noise. If we are primarily concerned with parties "getting on with their lives," this disregard for the law may be fine. But if family law is supposed to effectuate justice by distributing resources in a manner that honors particular sacrifices or marital commitments even when the parties do not, the decreasing relevance of law must be viewed as a potential problem.

The marital dissolution rules and procedures usually do not apply to unmarried couples. The more conventionally an unmarried couple lives — monogamously, with joint bank accounts and shared social lives — the more a court is likely to use notions of implicit contract or constructive trust or partnership theory to divide assets and possibly future income. But the court will rarely apply the property dissolution or alimony rules *per se*. Courts will usually enforce explicit contracts between unmarried cohabitants, but that is private parties dividing their assets, not the law determining who is entitled to what.

C. FAMILY REORGANIZATION FOR CHILDREN

In this final section, we will discuss the consequences of familial dissolution or reorganization for children. Recall that an agreement or contract was the root of the many theories for winding up affairs between adults. We ask what adults expected from each other, what they agreed to, and what implicit bargains might be gleaned from their conduct. By contrast, children are volunteers for nothing — not the choice of adult in their lives, not the fact of their dependency, not the financial stability of their household. The most important matters in a child's life are not of his or her choosing. The theory for creating adult obligations to children derives in part from the decisions adults make to become parents. But that justification combines with the bare dependency that is childhood, and that necessity relaxes the state's vigilance in theorizing the obligations it will impose to meet the needs of children. The state struggles with what parents deserve in return for their obligations to children — how their commitment should be honored — as well as what parents need from the law to be effective in their work. But the basic premise in responding to children is that the state may act in their best interest because they are dependent by definition. That justification informs the contours and limits of the state's role at the dissolution of family ties. But that state role is substantial. Children are usually not separately represented if their parents divorce. It is adults — parents and judges — who make decisions for them. We begin with the issues that confront children of divorce, and then we turn to children whose ties to their parents are involuntarily terminated by the state.

1. Child Support

The contemporary child support statutes reflect a wholesale rejection of the contemporary approach to alimony. The alimony debate bubbles with different theories of entitlement that in practice lead to disparate awards that reflect the wide variety of circumstances that accompany divorce. But child support awards are set by one of only two formulas that give the judge almost no discretion. (One state, Delaware, has a complicated third formula attempting to merge the theories behind the other two formulas.)

One nationwide model uses the *payor-only* or *percentage of income* formula. The child support payor is required to pay a set percentage of his net income depending on how many children he supports. For example, he might pay 20 percent for one child, 28 percent for two children, and 32 percent for three children. These percentages are set using economic methodologies that measure the marginal cost of raising children. A notable attribute of this formula is that the percentage paid stays the same whether the recipient, who is the child's other parent, has no income of her own and therefore great need or instead has a large income and little need.

The alternative model is called the *income-shares* formula. It adds together the incomes of both parents, and using the same economic models as the payor-only model, determines the marginal amount that an intact household consisting of those two parents would probably spend on a child. It allocates that sum between the parents in proportion to their percentage of the combined parental income. The noncustodial spouse has to pay the custodial spouse for just his share of a sum that takes into account the wealth of both parents. This formula not only recognizes that the custodial parent probably has an income, but the amount reflects the *relative* income of the two parents. In most instances the different formulas give comparable awards. However, as guidelines operate in practice, income-share states better recognize the need to distribute child-care costs.

Unlike most ex-spouses, children are entitled to a share of a parent's income because of their status as children, nothing more. Moreover, much of the legal rhetoric in this area suggests that children should be entitled to live at or very close to the standard of living established while the family was together, in part because they are blameless in the family dissolution. Indeed, the political allegiance to this belief suggests widespread failure to recognize the economies of scale that are inevitably lost when one household becomes two.

To accomplish the goal of minimizing a child's loss, as suggested, both the payor-only and the income-shares formula rely on econometric models that predict the marginal cost of raising a child. The *marginal cost of a child* is defined as the added amount a couple needs to spend each month once a new child arrives. The formulas recognize that each new child adds fewer expenses than the first child, and so the additional percentage added per child will be less than the amount for the first child.

There are several well-known flaws with using this measurement as the basis for child support. First, the marginal cost of a child to a two-parent household will be different than the marginal cost of a child to a one-parent household. Because of the economies of scale involved in living together, the two-parent household is able to provide services and goods to a child that will cost a single parent more. Child care and a car are examples of a service and a good that may be shared by a couple with a child. A single parent needs to buy more child care and may need to buy a car once a child arrives. The formulas ignore these added costs of divorce. Second, the marginal-cost methodology assumes that the custodial spouse should pay completely for any items jointly consumed by her and her children, such as utilities and rent, because she would have these expenses even without the child. This means that a payor spouse is not responsible for any of his child's rent or utility costs.

Notwithstanding these limitations, the formulas do an adequate job of equalizing the income level between custodial and noncustodial households if the parents earn approximately the same amount of money. The child will not achieve the ideal of enjoying the marital standard of living, but at least the child enjoys the same standard of living as both parents. Because of the flaws mentioned above, however, the formulas do a poor job of equalizing the standard of living between the households if one parent makes substantially more than the other. Where the spousal earnings are unequal, the higher earning spouse's standard of living will rise postdivorce relative to the lower earning spouse, at least if the transfer payments are limited to child support and do not include substantial alimony.

An example may best explain this issue. Assume a two-parent household with a combined net income of $100,000, with the marginal cost of one child at $20,000. If both spouses earn $50,000, then under a single-payor formula, the noncustodial spouse will pay the custodial spouse 20 percent of his net income, or $10,000. Under an income-shares formula, the noncustodial spouse will pay the same $10,000, which will reflect his share (50 percent) of the marginal cost of the child ($20,000). In both cases, the custodial household, made up of parent and child, will live on $60,000 a year. The noncustodial household, made up of just one parent, will live on $40,000 a year.

Consider what happens if the earnings differential is much greater. Suppose the noncustodial spouse earns $80,000 a year and the custodial spouse earns $20,000 a year. The marginal cost of the child would still be $20,000. Under the single-payor formula, the noncustodial spouse would pay 20 percent of his $80,000, or $16,000. Under the income shares formula, he would pay his share (80 percent) of the marginal cost, or, again, $16,000. In either case, the custodial household, made up of parent and child, would be living on $36,000 a year, while the noncustodial household made up of just one parent would be living on $64,000 a year.

A further theoretical flaw with both formulas is that their baseline is a two-parent household. Thirty percent of the children in this country are born to single mothers, and millions more children and parents live in a blended family at some point. Less than half of American children spend their entire childhood in a household consisting only of their married parents and legal siblings. Thus, the child support formula is based on a model that for many parents and children never existed. Even if it did, it has questionable relevance to the economic situation in which payor, payee, and child find themselves for most of the childhood at issue. Once again, we see the power of the normative traditional nuclear family. It defines all children's entitlements, even though most children probably experience it for part of their childhood only, if at all.

Nonetheless, the child support formulas are relatively uncontroversial and quite popular. Compared to what predated them, they are wildly successful. After decades of erratic, confused, and chronically low child support awards, reform movements in the 1980s sought to ensure that children would receive a reasonable amount of money in a reliable manner. The current formulas meet that goal. Judges know exactly what to award; they just plug income numbers into a formula. Because the formulas are so rigid, claims for exceptions and exemptions and hardship get very little traction. Exceptions are granted if parental income levels are extraordinarily high; if the child has substantial sources of independent income as from a trust, for instance; or if the child has unusual needs arising from disability or illness; but the exceptions are few and far between.

The federal government also plays a substantial role in ensuring the child support formulas' success. Due mostly to the increased federalization of social welfare policy that began in the 1960s, the federal government acquired a keen interest in finding alternative sources of income for low-income women and children. By the early 1980s, the federal government was concerned with naming, finding, and requiring payment from fathers. Congress passed two different Child Support Acts in the 1980s. These were aimed at collecting child support from fathers of children who were receiving welfare payments, thereby decreasing the children's need for government support. The first law required all states to develop specific numerical child support guidelines that took into account the earnings and income of the noncustodial parent. The second required that those guidelines act as rebuttable presumptions for an award. Prior to that federal mandate, awards had been discretionary, in just the way they are now for alimony. Federal legislation transformed child support from an unreliable, occasional, inconsistent order to a widespread entitlement routinely and consistently ordered.

In addition, federal law made it easier for state enforcement agencies to garnish wages, withhold drivers' licenses, and otherwise collect payments from recalcitrant payors. The direct beneficiaries of these policies were the federal and state governments who could reduce payments to women and children. But the entitlement to a child support award became universal and reached beyond women on public assistance. The indirect beneficiaries of these policies were divorced or never-married middle- and upper-middle-class women and children. Their ability to rely on child support payments has grown increasingly realistic with every federal government initiative. The federal legislation may have been designed with potential welfare recipients in mind, but the mandates transformed child support law regardless of class. Despite longstanding doctrines suggesting that family law is a matter for state, not federal, law, the last

30 years of child support enforcement reveal a constant, significant, and effective federal role in ensuring that children receive support from their legal parents.

The child support formulas put a premium on simplicity and consistency, but their failure to consider context sometimes leads to curious results. The child's entitlement is a function of what a parent has, not what the child needs. As the alimony discussion suggested, determining need can be extremely difficult. But a refusal to consider need means that the child born of a brief fling with a rich man can be entitled to a child support payment that is hundreds of times greater than his half-brother, even though the two brothers may share a bedroom in the custodial mother's home. Each father typically pays 20 percent of his income. Also, the child support formulas are ill-equipped to deal with the most prevalent living arrangements encountered by children of divorce today: blended households that include numerous sources of income and a variety of different people of all ages sharing many household goods.

More fundamentally, the child support formulas apply to all parents regardless of how they became parents or what they agreed to. A divorced man who eagerly wanted children, actively parented them, and participates in the major decision making for the child's life owes the same amount as a comparably earning man whose birth control failed in a one-night stand or whose girlfriend lied to him about birth control. It is legal parenthood, not volitional parenthood or context, that determines obligation. The extent of the obligation is determined by an income formula, not by a balancing of the equities and interests among the adults. A modest measure of regard for children and child welfare probably creates tolerance for this lack of context. The varied and highly contested theories of alimony suggest that when children are not involved, the law pays much closer attention to context. The foundation of the obligation among adults is some agreement between them, so the equities between them matter. The foundation of the obligation to children is not negotiation but derives from their natural dependency. That dependency doesn't determine where obligation lies, but it does structure the issue.

The duty to support one's children usually lasts until the child reaches age 18, but sometimes it lasts longer. No state requires the use of child support formulas after age 18, but many states require a noncustodial parent to contribute to the cost of postsecondary education. Orders of this kind are most common among middle- and upper-income families for whom college is considered a standard part of children's educational paths. The orders are justified on the theory that almost all residential parents contribute to postsecondary educational costs and therefore nonresidential parents should bear the same burden. Children of non-normative homes should receive what children who live the normative ideal receive. A handful of states reject imposing this additional burden on noncustodial parents because no state compels married parents to contribute to their children's educational expenses.

Judicially ordered support of post-secondary education is a clear example of divorced parents losing liberties that are otherwise at the core of their constitutional rights as parents. In this case, those liberties are curtailed in favor of providing to children of divorce what most children receive in married families. Married parents have complete discretion over what they will spend on education and how they will structure their financial support. Despite that discretion, married parents rarely choose to deny all financial assistance to college-aged children if they have the means to provide for them. In a contest of values between supporting children as they likely would be in an intact family and parental decision-making authority granted to intact families, the former wins. Although higher-education expenses illustrate this contest, it is a more general dilemma of child support orders. Married parents may always choose to minimally support children in their own home

158

at a lower percentage of their income than the average marginal cost figures used in child support guidelines.

The justification for this disparate treatment of divorced and married parents lies in the same policy that generated the rigid child support guidelines: Children whose parents do not live together should suffer as little as possible because of that separation. Children do not choose their parents' relationship status, and the law benchmarks their entitlement to the normative nuclear family, regardless of its likelihood. Choosing this benchmark hypothesizes the most secure financial arrangement their parents could theoretically have had. It does not matter if the parents never really were together, and it does not matter if the parents would have provided less even if they were together. A little too much upon occasion is thought a reasonable price to pay for a comprehensive, reliable child support policy that ensures a sizable transfer of funds from parents to children.

2. Custody

Custody may be the most contentious issue in divorce today because so much of the acrimony over other matters in dispute has been reduced. With no-fault rules, marital transgressions are rarely relevant. With property distribution, an equal-sharing principle operates as a presumption or starting point, and in many cases arguing for deviation is unproductive. With alimony, short-term awards are easily negotiated, and the principles are sufficiently contested for longer-term awards that many parties forego a sustained fight for it.[6] Fights over child support are rare for the opposite reason: The guidelines leave no discretion or room for party input.

Like child support, custody awards have to be made in every case involving children. But like alimony, there is very little implicit or explicit baseline allocation or formula to help judges determine how parents should share custodial rights. Instead, almost every state requires that custody determinations be made under a *best interest of the child* standard (BIOC). BIOC is so opaque and discretionary that it can support almost any argument. The combination of a capacious custody standard and an end to fault inquiries at divorce has led some scholars to conclude that custody determination is now the moral fulcrum of family law adjudication. The no-fault mentality reduces the inclination to label adults as bad spouses. But the custody standards may encourage one litigant to frame the other as a bad parent.

Indeterminate custody standards centered on the quality of parenting are a modern invention. For most of Western European history, and extant in much of the world with strong patriarchal cultures, the father retained custody of any child of divorce. By the nineteenth century in this country, most states shifted to the opposite, bright-line maternal preference rule, at least for young children. Originally, regard for mothers influenced the adoption of this *tender-years doctrine*. The maternal presumption operated well into the 1960s in many states, although by that time it was justified as serving children's needs rather than adults'. By the 1970s the tender-years doctrine had been replaced by the gender-neutral BIOC standard.

The widespread adoption of the BIOC standard was fueled by notions of gender equality, but its ubiquity may also be a function of its facial appeal to children's well-being. Few people want to argue against a standard designed to protect children's best interest. But as we will see, many times judges do not know what is in children's best interest, or they are powerless to protect that interest even if they can determine it. Moreover, sometimes a parent's investment in parenting (or lack thereof) may seem important in a custody determination even if parental behavior is not obviously pertinent to an evaluation of the child's best interests.

Initially, a common custody order emerged under the BIOC standard, though each judge was supposed to evaluate every case *de novo*. Typically, the mother received primary custody, with all major decision-making authority, and the father received visitation of one weeknight a week and a 24-hour stretch on the weekends (or every other weekend). This common award was never described in statute but was regarded by many judges as appropriate across numerous factual scenarios. In practice, awards were not very different than they had been under the tender-years doctrine.

It is not clear exactly why judges believed that this allocation of custody was in the best interest of children or if, indeed, they even thought about whether it was in children's best interest. It may have been that (1) many judges believed that mothers are inherently better at nurturing and raising children than are men; (2) most mothers did much more caretaking of children than most fathers, and therefore the mothers in the judges' courtrooms appeared to be more expert at child care than did the fathers; (3) most fathers spent more hours each week in the workforce and therefore were less available for their children; or (4) fathers did not want custody. The first of these hypotheses was probably a constitutionally impermissible basis for a custody award, at least by the mid-1970s. Reasons 2 and 3 suggest that even as the best-interest standard was adopted to rid the law of gender stereotypes, gender norms remained. Courts eventually eliminated the tender-years presumption as a matter of equality doctrine. But the gender norms that thrive outside the law and inside families initially made the elimination of that doctrine inconsequential to custody outcomes.

Studies confirm the fourth hypothesis: Men rarely asked for custody. Consequently, judges spent very little time evaluating what was in children's best interest, because they were not asked to. Children went with the mothers because everybody assumed that would happen. Before the child support reforms of the 1980s, which made awards more common, substantial, and collectible, this often meant that the mother and children had limited access to the father's resources or his person.

In 1973, a highly influential book, *Beyond the Best Interest of the Child*, helped explain why maternal custody might be in the best interest of children. Written by Anna Freud, a child analyst, Joseph Goldstein, a law professor, and Albert Solnit, a psychiatrist, the book argued that a continuing, consistent adult presence in a child's life is critical for that child's self-esteem. Postdivorce, it is in the best interest of children to have one primary caretaker. All child-rearing authority should be vested in that primary adult. Split authority could lead to detrimental confusion, inconsistency, and tension for the child. Their argument suggested that the best-interest standard is coterminous with a primary-caretaker standard, because the parent who has been the main source of emotional support and authority before divorce should remain as such postdivorce. Practically speaking, it is the mother in most families who has played that role, regardless of her participation in the paid labor force. A few states have adopted a primary-caretaker standard in place of the BIOC standard, and most statutes list the primary caretaker as one factor that should go into a best-interest inquiry.

The maternally favored custody allocation that Freud, Goldstein, and Solnit seemed to favor is not as common today as it once was, notwithstanding the fact that women still do the vast majority of unpaid caretaking. The noncustodial parent now gets more custodial time and much more decision-making authority than in the past. Perhaps the increase in men's caretaking in recent years changed minds about the propriety of men caring for children, even granting that they still do less than women. Perhaps men realize that the child support formulas preclude reducing child support through litigation, so the battle has shifted to custody. Perhaps there is an increasing belief that an ideal custody allocation involves substantial sharing between mothers and fathers, what is legally known as *joint custody*. Whatever the reason, Freud, Goldstein, and Solnit's call for unitary authority could not withstand the pressure to expand men's parental rights.

The same push for gender equality that helped eliminate the tender-years presumption generated the idea of joint custody. If there really were no material differences between mothers and fathers, then they should share custody after divorce evenly. This ideal found support among some feminists who wanted to de-gender caretaking, as well as among some men who were angry because they felt shut out of parenthood. Whether joint custody is good for children is another question. If we believe that it is best for children to rear them in a world without rigid gender roles, then a joint custody standard makes sense. If we believe that stability and consistency of parental care allows children to thrive, then joint custody may be too cumbersome. The ideal may be a child-rearing regime that minimizes gender roles and maximizes consistency, but that may not be possible in most cases.

One exercise that can help people to appreciate the challenges of joint custody from a child's perspective is to imagine a similar arrangement for adults. There is an uncommon custody arrangement called *bird nesting*, in which children stay in the same house and parents move in and out over the course of a week depending on who has custody on a given day. This allows children the benefits of joint custody — ongoing substantial residential relationships with both parents — without imposing the disruption of regular moving that falls to children in many joint custody arrangements. Most people immediately feel that it would be intolerable to ask parents to trade houses on a weekly basis. But that is what joint custody arrangements ask of children. It is for this reason that some argue joint physical custody meets the needs and rights of parents better than those of children. Perhaps children really are more flexible and adaptable than adults, or perhaps they are not but lack the power to control their level of stability.

A few states adopted a presumption of joint custody in the 1980s. Other states suggested that it was an outcome that judges should consider. In the vast majority of cases, however, full joint physical custody is infeasible. Often, one of the parents does not want the responsibility of providing care and nurturance of a child or children 50 percent of the time. In other cases, it is economically or practically difficult to provide two separate homes, each close enough to the child's school and other activities for the child to feel fully at home in both places.

One way that legislatures tried to reconcile the ideals of joint custody with its practical difficulties was to start disaggregating the term *custody* itself. At one time, an award of custody bestowed exclusive parental rights, including the exclusive right to make all decisions on behalf of the child. By the late 1980s courts began distinguishing between legal custody — meaning the right to make decisions on behalf of the child, from physical custody, meaning residential and custodial time with the child. Joint legal custody is now the default rule in most jurisdictions. As a practical matter, the parent with more physical custody makes more decisions on behalf of a child, because many of those decisions must be made on an immediate basis. But many other major decisions, such as the choice of school, medical care, or extracurricular activities to participate in, can be shared between divorced parents.

Sharing responsibility for children requires a degree of cooperation and contact that complicates a clean-break severance of the adults' attachment to each other. The emerging notions of gender equality that undermined women's claims to postdivorce support from men were thought to let the parties go separate ways after divorce. But not if there are children involved. Those same notions of gender equality support a more mutual allocation of parental rights and thus a greater degree of postdivorce interaction between the spouses.

This interaction comes with costs, and at time those costs are high enough that we should probably be wary of any joint legal custody presumption. For instance, a parent with a history of domestic violence against his spouse is not necessarily disqualified from receiving a joint custody award. If it is in the children's interest to interact substantially with both parents, courts will make the custody joint. The only way to combat such a ruling is to indicate that the former abuse could so substantially interfere with the parents' ability to cooperate that joint custody will not work. But alleging abuse is different than proving abuse, and a spouse who alleges it without being able to prove it runs the risk of being accused of lack of cooperation herself. It is often very difficult to prove past abuse if the injuries have healed and the violence took place in private, without witnesses. An inadequately corroborated allegation of abuse can turn the abused parent into a "bad," "noncooperative" parent in the court's eyes.

It is not only previously violent marriages that appear to be bad candidates for joint custody. High-conflict divorces, in which the spouses demonstrate an incapability of respecting or cooperating with each other, can lead to bad joint custody outcomes. There is some evidence that courts are even more likely to award joint custody in these cases because the recalcitrance from both parties is so intense that courts do not know how to resolve the custody question. No outcome seems to be in the children's best interest. So some judges award joint custody as a way of forcing the parties to work it out. But the parents rarely do so amicably, and this can leave children wounded as they are forced to watch their parents engage in viscious and recurring battles.

Even when courts award joint legal custody, they must determine the amount of physical custody that each parent gets. The BIOC standard leaves ample room for contestable issues that make custody allocations complicated. First there is the theoretical debate over the importance of a primary caretaker relationship. If a mother spending more time caring for the child during marriage leads to an award of more custodial time with the child, is that for the child's benefit or because it is fair to the mother in light of her investment? If the latter concern plays a role, then a BIOC standard is not being used.

Many scholars also question whether judges are capable of determining what is in a child's best interest in a non-arbitrary fashion, without incorporating their own class, ethnic, and personal biases. A judge's ideals of childhood may reflect what he experienced as a child. If confronted with a childhood that looks different, he may assume it is inferior. How should a judge balance a child's need for stability against the offsetting advantages that may become available when a noncustodial parent remarries and can provide the child with all the trappings of a "traditional" home? Judges have no training to make those psychological judgments — they are equipped to apply legal standards. To aid them in the decision-making process, judges and the lawyers often enlist guardians *ad litem* and other professional psychological experts. Guardians *ad litem* and psychologists may not be accustomed to using due process norms that would help them to avoid illegal or inappropriate bases for their opinions. In the end, the judge must evaluate the battle of the experts.

In addition, there are the problems associated with open-ended standards in general. Because the BIOC standard is so capacious, almost any argument can be made under its umbrella. This means that virtually anyone who wants a fight can have one. There are many advantages to legal standards that operate as bright-line rules, not open-ended ones, because bright-line rules decrease the incentive to litigate. On the other hand, critics of bright-line rules argue that they prevent consideration of context and particularities that lead to more equitable results. Because there are children involved in custody determinations, some people think that case-by-case attention to context and particularities is critical. But the argument for bright-line rules in the custody context is particularly compelling as well. Not only does litigation tap resources from the parties that would otherwise be available for children, it tends to breed greater animosity between the parties. Sustained animosity between parents reliably predicts bad outcomes for children of divorce. Moreover, when children are in middle school and older, litigation often forces the child to formulate and express a view about her preferred custody arrangement. This process may lead her to take on feelings of guilt or to act to protect a vulnerable parent rather than her own interests.

The American Law Institute's response to the problems with the best-interest standard is to suggest a baseline formula of sorts: "the proportion of custodial time the child spends with each parent [should] approximate the proportion of time each parent spent performing caretaking functions for the child prior to the parents' separation." In other words, the past should decide the future. But divisions of caretaking that may have worked when the parents lived together can be completely infeasible when the parties live apart. Many breadwinner spouses feel they have sacrificed time with their children in order to work to support them financially, and that sacrifice should not be held against them in determining time with their children in the new postdivorce lifestyle. In addition, many of the practical problems associated with joint physical custody attend a custodial plan based on past behavior. It is much easier to trade off time when everyone is living in the same home.

Postdivorce custodial arrangements can also last much longer than the pre-divorce caretaking arrangement did. Because courts retain jurisdiction over children of divorce until the children are 18 years old, the best-interest question can be continually reevaluated. The BIOC standard gives each parent the ongoing right to question the other parent's practices before a judge, even where those practices are well above the standard needed to preserve privacy against child welfare intervention. In theory, the judge is obliged to review the child's situation and make sure it is in accord with the child's best interests. There are several issues that commonly arise, and courts have had to develop methods of evaluating them under the BIOC standard.

a. Adult Sexual Behavior

One of the ideals of no-fault reform was to let the parties go their separate ways. This principle anticipates subsequent romantic relationships. For years, though, courts had doubts about the propriety of allowing a custodial parent, usually the woman, to engage in any kind of sexual relationship that the children might be exposed to. Up through much of the 1980s, courts would frequently reallocate custody because a mother allowed a man to spend the night in her bedroom when the children were in the home. Sometimes, courts made custody allocation contingent on the mother refraining from that conduct again. Fathers were not subject to the same regulation of their postdivorce sex lives, in large part because their children were not around them.

In most states, restrictions of this sort have lessened. Usually, a court will amend a custody order only if there is a strong indication that children are harmed by the custodial parent's conduct. The movement toward this *harm principle* suggests growing judicial caution when it comes to applying the BIOC standard. Increasingly, courts refuse to change the status quo allotment of custody, unless there is concrete evidence of harm. Harm is often difficult to prove, particularly in the short term. Judges are wary of assuming that they can determine what is in the child's best interest, so they let the status quo govern.

The one exception to this rule, in some states, involves same-sex relationships. Some judges still discourage a parent from conducting a same-sex relationship in a child's presence. They occasionally condition custodial or visitation time on not exposing the child to any physical contact with a same-sex partner, even a kiss. Conversely, many other states openly endorse gay parenting, and in those states one does not see this monitoring of sexual activity in the name of protecting the child.

b. Religion

Many parental rights that seemed sacrosanct when a couple is married disappear when they get divorced. Married parents have the right to raise a child in whatever religious tradition they want. The state does not interfere with that choice. Once parents are divorced, however, each acquires the right to challenge the other's decision with regard to religious exposure. The harm principle has emerged here also as the guiding rule when one parent takes issue with the religious training provided by the other parent. Two parents from different faith traditions who, while married, may have enjoyed what seemed like a culturally rich household (or conversely experienced conflict over religion) often fail to see the virtue in the other's religious traditions once divorced. Under the BIOC standard, a parent can invite a judge to evaluate the other parent's religious behavior. The child's best interest, even if a judge felt confident that she could determine it, must be balanced against the parent's free exercise right. Free exercise usually wins, unless one party can show that the child is being harmed by a certain kind of religious exposure. Again, proving harm in this context can be difficult.

When they cannot prove harm, parents sometimes resort to a kind of religious counterattack, with the child at the center. Parental free exercise rights are understood to include a right to inculcate one's children with one's religious values. Each parent is free to inculcate on his or her own time. This can leave the child exposed to a kind of free market of religious ideas run amuck. Parents can escalate their own religious dedication and expose their children to any kind of extremity, including claims that the other parent is eternally condemned. That can be a disturbing notion for the child. It's hard to see how that kind of religious competition is in the child's best interest, but it may be too hard to formulate an intervention standard that avoids impermissibly restricting parents' constitutional rights. Upon occasion, courts have intervened in the battle for the child's soul by awarding "spiritual" or "religious" custody to one party. Religious custody requires the other parent to facilitate the chosen religion even when he or she has visitation and not to overexpose the children to alternatives.

c. Relocation

The hottest topic in custody law today is relocation. In an increasingly mobile society, it is likely that divorced parents will want to move away from each other for a variety of legitimate reasons, including a new job, familial support, or a new spouse. The court must decide if a spouse who wants to move may move the child with her, and whether the inevitable impact on the other spouse's custodial time is permissible.

Over the years, states have taken a variety of approaches to this issue. Some worked from a presumption that a move was in the child's best interest, while others worked from the opposite presumption. Whoever had the burden usually won, because the parties' interests usually balanced each other out. The moving spouse is benefited by the move, while the nonmoving spouse's parental interest in companionship with his child is hurt by the move. The child is helped to the extent that the moving spouse is happier, wealthier, and/or more supported and hurt to the extent that his relationship with the nonmoving spouse will be strained. The BIOC standard was not capable of deciding these questions.

The last ten years have seen recognition of the inadequacy of the BIOC standard in these contexts. Accordingly, a general rule of *reasonableness* has emerged. Most moves will be allowed as long as there is a practical, economically feasible way of allowing the nonmoving parent to maintain a reasonable amount of contact with the child. Some courts do a cursory examination of the moving parent's reasons for the move as well. Although early cases required a very good reason for the move, the trend has been sharply away from changing custody based on a custodial parent's move.

3. Visitation and Third-party Rights

For years, visitation was treated as a consolation prize when it was awarded to a parent who would have preferred physical custody. Even the parent who did not seek custody got visitation. Visitation involved no parental decision-making functions and usually not much time, either. Most states today have a strong presumption in favor of some visitation for all legal parents, even if those parents have marginal parenting experience or skills. As the name suggests, a person with visitation rights is not given the right to raise the child. He or she is given the right to visit with the child periodically. More than a few jurisdictions have now eliminated the term *visitation* as applied to parents because it makes one parent sound like an outsider to the child's life. Parents are more likely to get something called a "parenting plan," delineating "custodial time." The nomenclature was changed in no small part to reduce the perception of "winners" and "losers" in custody determinations.

Visitation as a term and a legal right has not disappeared, however. Instead, there are new classes of people getting it. Relationship rights with children allow a court to order a parent to let another adult spend time with a child. Traditionally those relationship rights were limited to other parents. Courts only imposed upon a custodial parent's rights in the name of vindicating the other parent's rights. No other family members, no other critical adults in children's lives could receive a court order. The one exception to this involved a doctrine known as the *in loco parentis* doctrine. An adult who acted as a primary parent could receive *in loco parentis* standing. That standing gave the *in loco* parent the right to petition for visitation. To secure visitation, the *in loco* parent had to overcome the presumption in favor of the legal parent's judgment as to who might visit with her child. Presumably, the legal parent did not want the *in loco* parent to have visitation, or there would be no need for the parties to be in court.

The most common situation in which this issue would arise involved stepparents. If a custodial parent remarried someone who developed strong relationships with the parent's children, but then the second marriage faltered, the stepparent could request from a court a visitation order with his or her stepchildren. The standing rules were so rigid, though, that to get the opportunity to be heard, the stepparent had to prove that the primary parent abdicated a substantial amount of his or her parental responsibility. The right of legal parents to control who saw their children and when was treated with so much deference that nonparents rarely got a chance to make their case.

Few states still adhere to these rigid standing rules. Indeed, several states now have statutes that allow *anyone* who can establish a strong relationship with the child to bring a claim arguing that visitation would be in the child's best interest. Most states have statutes guaranteeing grandparents the right to petition for visitation. Many states provide the same protection for stepparents. In all of these cases, the petitioners must overcome a presumption that the parent's desire to exclude them from contact should govern; standing does not mean the routine order of visitation. The U.S. Supreme Court upheld a parent's right to that presumption in *Troxel v. Granville*,[7] but it is now much easier for someone wanting visitation rights to make an argument for them.

What happened? The expansion of visitation rights is probably attributable to the rise of varied household compositions and the decreasingly rigid social norms that govern how children are to be raised, particularly among middle-class families. Lower-income parents have always raised children in homes with extended relatives and non-relatives, sometimes because exigency dictated that households be shared. A variety of different adults have often played a role in raising the children in low-income households. But rarely did people in those households have the resources to sue in court if some adult felt she was being unfairly deprived of a relationship with the child.

Those kinds of varied household arrangements are now more common among people with greater resources. There are more divorced parents with children, and those divorced parents often cohabit with other adults. Divorced or never-married parents move back in with their parents or they ask their parent(s) to move in with them. Parents often rely extensively on their siblings or friends for child care. Adults routinely develop strong emotional bonds with children who are not, in the legal sense, "theirs." Visitation rules provide these adults with a means of having a court enforce an order that gives them an opportunity to maintain those bonds even after rapport between the adults has disintegrated. (The court cannot ensure that the bond is maintained because that is a function of the interpersonal dynamic between child and adult.)

These visitation rules are most important for two very different constituencies: grandparents and same sex partners. Largely owing to the lobbying strength of the American Association of Retired People (AARP), grandparents have secured statutory rights to visitation in some cases even if they have no strong preexisting relationship with a child. In some states, grandparents can assert this right regardless of whether the child's parents are married. In practice, and by statute in some states, grandparents have a claim to visitation only if one of the parents is dead or missing—the one who is their own child and would presumably have protected their grandparental rights. If neither parent, both of whom are entitled to a presumption that they act in the best interest of the child, wants the grandparent to visit, it is highly unlikely that the grandparent will be able to overcome that double presumption against visitation. The parental entitlements to presumptions that they are acting in the child's best interest cancel each other out when the parents are fighting with each other, but not when they are fighting with non-parents. When one parent is missing, however, many grandparents have overcome the parental presumption and won for themselves the right to visitation.

The other group for whom visitation rights have proved to be particularly important are nonbiological gay and lesbian parents. With the increased acceptance and availability of gamete donation, there has been a great increase in the number of gay and lesbian people who either get pregnant or enter into surrogacy arrangements, planning to raise a child without the other genetic parent. Often, however, these parents plan to or end up raising the child with a partner. The emerging cases in states with gay marriage or civil union status suggest that non-biological parents have a marital presumption that treats them as a full legal parent. In some states regardless of whether the state grants same sex marriage or civil union statute, the non-biological parent can adopt the child and obtain full legal status as a parent (see second parent adoption discussion, *supra*). But if the nongenetic parent is not entitled to a presumption of parenthood or has not adopted, he or she is a legal stranger to the child. If the couple breaks up and the genetic parent wants to exclude the other parent, the nonbiological parent can be left without any legal claim to relationship rights with a child.

Because many states have significantly loosened their standing rules, however, many courts will grant standing based on a best interest of the child inquiry. The court can decide that, given the child's relationship with the nonlegal parent, it would be in the child's best interest for the court to determine whether that non-legal parent should receive relationship rights. In granting these rights, courts often look to the intent of the parties, as they do when determining parenthood in cases involving reproductive technologies. If the parties intended to share parenting rights and duties, courts will often grant standing to the nonlegal or nonbiological, yet intended, parent. The best way to ensure evidence of this kind of intent is with written documents indicating the legal parent's desire to share. Once standing is granted, the non-legal parent can make a claim for custody or visitation, but she is much more likely to get visitation. She gets the consolation prize. But the connotation of "winners" and "losers" associated with visitation may be seen as less problematic when the adults are not similarly situated as legal parents.

Often, courts refer to these nonbiological and nonlegal parents as *de facto parents*, and the class is not limited to gay partners. Straight people who have shared parenting duties, aunts and uncles who have assumed parenting responsibilities, and almost any other adult who has played a significant, ongoing role in a child's life can attempt to gain standing to make a visitation claim as a *de facto* parent. States vary in their receptivity to *de facto* parent claims, but today virtually all courts are more comfortable than they were 40 years ago abrogating a legal parent's rights by granting visitation to a non-parent.

The ALI Principles expressly provide a *de facto* parent doctrine that allows people who have spent a substantial amount of time caretaking for a child the right to petition for visitation. The ALI Principles refer to it as "custodial responsibility," not visitation. The degree of involvement of the nonbiological parent dictates the extent of the visitation award. If the non-biological parent has done the majority of the caretaking for the child, some courts are willing to grant full custodial rights, while others give only visitation. One class of people that is categorically denied standing is those who have received payment for their caretaking, such as a babysitter. The ALI and the courts use the receipt of payment as a reason to deny standing for visitation.

Even if less weighty than custodial rights, visitation rights should not be dismissed as unimportant. They can override a custodial parent's desire to move away if moving would completely eviscerate the visitor's relationship opportunity. They can allow the child to be subject to religious beliefs and practices or other values that the parent would rather the child not see. Particularly since petitioners are at odds with the primary parent as evidenced by the need to get a court order to see the child, visitation affords an adult the ability to say things that the primary parent considers disruptive, inappropriate, mean, or worse. The expansion of visitation rights to grandparents, stepparents, and other adults who have cared for children clearly marks a shift away from a strong parental rights ideology.

4. Termination of Parental Rights

Children whose parents and de facto parents fight with each other over custody and visitation issues often suffer because of the conflict. But they do not suffer nearly as much as children whose parents fight with the state over their very right to remain parents. As discussed in Chapter 3, the child welfare agency plays a role in an ongoing family, but it also plays a role in ending the family relationship between a parent and child if the agency thinks it necessary. To place a child for adoption, providing the child with a new permanent family, the legal rights of the first parents must be terminated. This is a drastic measure that permanently severs the relationship between parent and child. It is irreversible. The rights of each to the other's company or contact or information disappear.

In appreciation of both the significance of parental rights and the gravity of their termination, the U.S. Supreme Court has decided that the state must meet a high standard of proof — clear and convincing evidence — in order to terminate parental rights.[8] But the Supreme Court did not prescribe what needs to be proved by clear and convincing evidence. It acknowledged that a standard in this case would be subjective, saying that proceedings to terminate parental rights "employ imprecise substantive standards." But, the Supreme Court has declined to require the appointment of legal counsel for indigent parents in a proceeding to terminate parental rights.[9] What is offered before parental rights may be terminated is the constitutional guarantee of a high standard of proof of a substantive standard determined at the state level, and no right to counsel. A typical standard might be that a child is *permanently neglected* and that a state has in fact made reasonable efforts at reunification, by offering services and support to parents, without successfully repairing the home.

There is always worry that an agency will seek the termination of parental rights because a child is in a foster care family and has begun to thrive there. The agency is not supposed to be judging whether a child's circumstances could be improved (many could) but instead whether the original family is safe enough for the return of the child. But being human, as child welfare workers are, it is sometimes difficult to separate the two ideas. Further, recall that we embrace a wide range of appropriate ways to raise children, in theory, when we carve out enormous parental prerogatives for decision making about child rearing. In the words of the U.S. Supreme Court, "Because parents subject to termination proceedings are often poor, uneducated, or members of minority groups, such proceedings are often vulnerable to judgments based on cultural or class bias."[10]

An ongoing concern in child welfare policy is that children tend to be deeply attached to their parents, whether they are neglectful or even abusive. The severing of that attachment is often unwelcome to children as well as to the parents. Some wonder if it is necessary to impose on children the experience of full abandonment that can come with the termination of parental rights in order to provide children in danger with permanency and stability. In addition, children may have difficulty attaching to their new family if it requires a complete betrayal on their part of their former one. Children may also feel abandoned themselves by the termination of parental rights. There has been debate over whether a mechanism could be developed for allowing adoption of children in need of services, such that new parents can be assured of their permanent place, while allowing some ongoing contact with former parents to reduce a child's feeling of abandonment.

The current system parallels the traditional rules of exclusive parenthood, which limited parental right of any sort to two and only two parents. Reformers argue that just as the law now enforces visitation rights for de facto parents and genetic parents who never intended to be legal parents, it could provide visitation alternatives for those who still love and are loved by their children but who cannot get past the minimal safety threshold for legal parenthood. The current system of complete termination does not countenance that arrangement, but only a complete estrangement between parent and child. The racial and cultural tensions around the child welfare system are magnified by what is at stake in removing children from a family and sometimes a cultural system, using state power, and causing further trauma to parents and children who are already traumatized by abuse or neglect itself. Some of this might be minimized if the state took a less absolute approach to the termination of parental rights, instead attempting to both provide permanency elsewhere and to allow for some continued contact with original families.

ENDNOTES

1. Usually, the statute lists a number of factors to be considered by the judge, including the length of the marriage; age, health, and occupation of the parties; station in life; liabilities and needs; contribution to the marital estate, either through market work or household labor; assets and liabilities, including sources of income and separate property; the behavior of the parties during the marriage; and employability.

2. 706 A.2d 1021 (Conn. Super. Ct. 1996).

3. 2008 WL 5062805 (Ill. App. Dist., 2008) (affirming trial court's ruling, No. 1-07-1799).

4. *Orr. v. Orr*, 440 U.S. 268 (1979).

5. See Lloyd Cohen, *Marriage, Divorce and Quasi-Rents: or "I Gave Him the Best Years of My Life,"* 16 J LEGAL STUD 267 (1987).

6. In a few states, nonbinding guidelines offer a starting point for alimony and guide expectations.

7. 530 U.S. 57 (2000).

8. *Santosky v. Kramer*, 455 U.S. 745 (1982).

9. *Lassiter v. Dept of Social Services*, 452 U.S. 18 (1981).

10. *Santosky*, 455 U.S. 745 (1982).

⌁ 5 ⌁

Conclusion

The student cannot understand family law simply by understanding cases, statutes, regulations, and constitutions. She must understand something about families as well, including sociology, culture, psychology, demography, history, economics and production, and biology. While family law at times engages actively in shaping the course of families, at other times it seems to try to simply respond constructively to the way people choose to live and to the way culture and society expect people to behave. We see family law at its most awkward, and most visible, when family practices are in transition, and family law is either slow to catch up or too quick to institutionalize changes that are still in the making.

Making matters more difficult, family practices are changing rapidly now. The student of family law must take care not to assume that he understands families based only on his own experience or those of people he knows. Underappreciated by many, family practices have always changed rapidly, or too rapidly, for many contemporaneous social critics to handle. There is no era of the "traditional" family. Some of the periods commonly thought to have been the most stable, such as the 1950s, in practice saw dramatic increases in extramarital sex, which may have contributed to family instability in the following decades. There's no century, or even period of decades, when you will not find prominent social critics bemoaning radical changes in family structure that threaten to ruin the family as they knew it. In each case, it is true that family practices and culture were transformed. Whether the family was ruined is a different question. The demise of families has not happened, only their transformation. The job of the family lawyer includes expecting change in social norms to be reflected in law and preparing for inevitable cross-currents in the culture and in legal doctrine.

Glossary

Adoption. The legal process pursuant to which the state terminates the parental rights and responsibilities of one parent or set of parents in a child and bestows those parental rights and responsibilities on another parent or set of parents.

ALI (American Law Institute). The American Law Institute is an association of lawyers, academics, and judges. In 2002, the ALI published a comprehensive assessment of many family law doctrines and offered principles pursuant to which legislatures could act in drafting family law legislation.

Alimony. *See* maintenance.

Annulment. An annulment renders void a previous marriage retroactive to its beginning, as if it had never occurred. Annulment of a prior marriage is sought because certain religious faiths prohibit divorced members from remarrying.

Arbitration. An alternative to divorce litigation, arbitration requires divorcing parties to present their claims to a third party arbitrator, who is not a judge, but who has the authority to divide marital assets, award maintenance (alimony) and determine child support. Some states require parties to arbitrate their divorce claims, but mandatory arbitration is not binding; the parties can retry their case in court if they wish to incur the expense. Voluntary arbitration may be binding.

Best Interest of the Child (BIOC). The legal standard pursuant to which courts decide the vast majority of questions pertaining to children. Married parents enjoy a presumption that they act in the best interest of their children, but judges routinely adjudicate disputes between nonmarried parents based on the judge's determination of what is in the best interest of the child.

Bigamy. The act of being married to two people at one time. Bigamy is a crime in all states.

Bilateral divorce. Divorce sought with the agreement of both spouses that the marriage should end. *See also* unilateral divorce.

Bird nesting. The practice, among divorced or never-married parents, of letting the children stay in one home while the parents take turns (daily, weekly, monthly or some combination) living with the children in that home.

Child Custody. The right to assume physical responsibility for and to make decisions on behalf of a child. *See also* custody.

Child in need of services. A term used to describe children whom the state determines are in danger of being abused or neglected if their household does not receive services from the state.

Child Protective Services. The state agencies charged with making sure that children are not in danger of being abused or neglected by their parents or legal guardians.

Child support. The resources one parent provides to another to defray the cost of their child's upbringing.

Child support formulas. Mathematical formulas used to determine how much child support parents owe to each other. Forty-nine of the 50 states use one of two child support formulas (Delaware uses its own). All child support formulas are based on econometric models that try to ascertain the marginal cost of a child to a two-parent household.

Civil union. A licensed status conferred by some states that provides all the rights and benefits of marriage. To date, civil unions are only available to same sex couples.

Collaborative divorce. A divorce litigation alternative that allows each party to retain counsel and negotiate a divorce settlement, but with a proviso that the lawyers used to negotiate the settlement will be barred from litigating if the parties cannot reach settlement. Collaborative divorce is meant to encourage attorneys and parties to settle in order to avoid the cost and emotional toll of litigation.

Common law marriage. A valid marriage status in ten states and the District of Columbia, and honored by many other states, based on a couple's conduct rather than a state license. These states will declare a couple married if they are legally able to be married, have cohabited, had an intent to be married, and held themselves out as married for a period of time.

Community property. All property and income earned by either spouse during a marriage in a community property state. Community property is jointly owned, from the moment it is acquired, by both parties to the marriage.

Community property states. States (AZ, CA, NM, NV, ID, LA, TX, WA, WI) that follow community property rules. Community property rules were imported from continental Europe and are most prevalent among Western states that were originally settled by the Spanish and the French.

Companionate marriage. A norm of marriage as an institution rooted first in friendship and love and freely chosen by the parties themselves. It is juxtaposed with marriage rooted first in reproduction, economic efficiency, or property consolidation among extended families.

Contribution-based maintenance. A maintenance (alimony) award based on a theory that the receiving spouse is entitled to a maintenance amount that compensates her for the contribution, financial or service-based, that she has made to the marriage.

Coverture. The legal disability that once prevented a married woman from entering into binding legal transactions (including owning property or contracting) because she was "covered" by her husband. No state follows the principles of coverture today.

Custody.

> **Joint.** The joint sharing of child custody. In its fullest sense, joint custody involves equally dividing the amount of time each parent spends with the child (joint physical custody) and cooperating on all major child-rearing decisions (joint legal custody).
>
> **Legal.** The right to make child-rearing decisions on behalf of a child.
>
> **Physical.** The right to be with and assume physical responsibility for a child.

De facto parent. An adult who is not a legal parent to a child but who has assumed partial or complete parental responsibility for the child and may, therefore, be awarded visitation (and sometimes custody).

Defense of Marriage Act (DOMA). The Defense of Marriage Act was signed by President Clinton in 1996 and restricts the federal definition of marriage to a union between a man and a woman. This has implications for, among other things, Social Security eligibility, income tax liability, and spousal status rights for any employee of the federal government. In addition, DOMA encourages states not to respect the marital determinations of other states.

Divorce. The judicial termination of a marriage.

Domestic partnership. A legal status conferred by a state, county or municipality that enumerates and confers some of the rights of marriage on a couple registered as domestic partners. Domestic partners are usually same sex couples, but in some places opposite-sex couples may register as domestic partners.

Domestic relations lawyer. A lawyer who specializes in the laws pertaining to family, with an emphasis on the laws of divorce, marital property distribution, spousal maintenance, child custody, child support, and adoption.

Duty of Services. Duties of work that one spouse owes another during marriage. Historically, only the wife had a duty of services. These included, *inter alia*, cleaning, cooking, caring for children and the infirm, and sexual relations.

Duty of Support. The duty to provide for one's spouse. Historically, only the husband had a duty of support. The term is sometimes used today to incorporate both support and services.

Earnings Statutes. State statutes passed in the middle and late nineteenth century that allowed married women to earn wages on their own.

Egg donor. A woman who undergoes a surgical procedure in which ovum are extracted from her body so that they can be used by others to help produce a child. Egg donors rarely "donate" their eggs; they are paid. Egg donors generally have no parental rights and responsibilities for any child conceived.

Equitable parenthood. A doctrine, akin to de facto parenthood, through which people who would not otherwise be considered legal parents are treated as parents because they have performed the duties of parent.

Fault-based divorce. Divorce that is granted after a court determines that the fault of one spouse caused the break-up of the marriage. Fault would be found on specific grounds, such as adultery, abandonment, or cruelty. At one time in this country all divorce was fault-based. Today, fault-based divorces are rare and many states have eliminated them completely.

Foregone opportunities. A theory pursuant to which a spouse is entitled to maintenance approximately equal to the amount she could be earning if she had not invested instead in the marriage and thereby foregone earning opportunities.

Gestational surrogate. A woman who contracts or otherwise agrees to have a fertilized egg implanted in her uterus so that she can gestate it and deliver it for someone else who wishes to be a parent.

Griswold. *Griswold v. Connecticut* is a significant case in which the U.S. Supreme Court first held that the Constitution protects a right to privacy and that a married couple enjoys that right to privacy. In *Griswold*, this right to privacy was held to prevent the state from regulating the distribution of contraceptives.

Guardian *ad litem*. A lawyer or social service specialist appointed by a court to represent the interests of a child in court. Guardians *ad litems* are used in some divorce cases and in most cases brought by Child Protective Services (see entry).

Homemaker. A family member whose occupation is unpaid labor and management for the family and its members.

Income shares formula. One of two primary child support formulas used by courts to determine child support amounts. The income shares formula adds both parents' incomes together and then assigns support responsibilities based on the percentage of the total income that each parent earns.

In loco parentis. A legal position of a nonparent adult who, often due to an institutional position, assumes some of the responsibilities of a temporarily absent parent. A person who has stood *in loco parentis* within a family may seek to establish some parental rights to visitation or custody of a child.

Intent to parent standard. A standard used to determine parenthood in cases using modern reproductive technologies. In most cases, regardless of the origins of the genetic material or gestational labor, the parties who demonstrated the *preconception* intent to parent the child are awarded parental rights and responsibilities.

In vitro fertilization. The process of fertilizing an egg with a sperm outside of a womb and then inserting the fertilized egg into a womb for gestation.

Irreconcilable differences. The statutory standard most courts use in determining whether to grant a no-fault divorce; the finding is now *pro forma*.

Legal guardian. An adult who is not a legal parent to a child, but who has been granted the legal right to assume parental rights and responsibilities.

Legal parent. An adult who is endowed with certain constitutional, statutory, and common law rights to rear a child and who is obliged to support the child financially.

Maintenance. Formerly called *alimony*, maintenance is a financial award to a divorcing spouse, entitling him or her to a share of the other spouse's future income stream, usually for a fixed period of time. Alimony was originally viewed as the post-separation extension of the husband's duty of support. Today, maintenance is more likely to be viewed as a theory of compensation for past contribution or entitlement based on reasonable reliance.

Marginal cost per child. An econometric measurement designed to ascertain the increased cost to a two-parent household, at any given income level, of an additional child.

Marital privacy. A doctrine protecting a married couples' privacy often used by courts to resist analyzing marital decision-making or power imbalances. *See also* noninterference doctrine.

Marital property. A concept applied only in noncommunity property states, marital property is the pool of property acquired by either spouse during a marriage. It is subject to distribution between the parties at divorce, regardless of who owns it, distinguishing it from separate property.

Marital roles. The tendency of married couples to divide labor and to specialize in different roles such as wage earner and provider, caretaker, consumer, homemaker, and financial planner. Marital roles have a strong tendency to track traditional gender roles.

Marital unity. Both an old common-law doctrine that treated the marital couple as one entity in which the husband had almost complete control (*see* coverture) and a more modern theory that endorses legal treatment of the couple as a unit and thereby discourages courts from analyzing too carefully individual behaviors within that unit.

Marriage. The status pursuant to which two people are treated as spouses by government and thereby acquire certain rights and obligations *vis a vis* each other and third parties. No more than two people can be married to each other legally. In most states, people of the same sex cannot be married to each other. Marriage is also a cultural, religious, and social institution celebrated and recognized by nongovernmental entities.

Married Women's Property Acts. State statutes passed in the middle and late nineteenth century that allowed women to own property on their own.

McGuire. *McGuire v. McGuire* is a 1953 Nebraska case in which the state Supreme Court refused to assume jurisdiction over a married woman's claim that her husband's duty of support included providing more for her, given his financial ability to do so. *McGuire* is understood as a paradigmatic example of the nonintervention doctrine (see below).

Mediation. An alternative to litigated divorce in which the divorcing parties negotiate a settlement in the presence of a neutral third party, who may or may not have legal training.

Meretricious relationship. A common law name for the relationship between two people who are not married but who have sexual relations.

Necessaries doctrine. A doctrine that allows one spouse's creditor to sue the other spouse for the cost of necessary items purchased on credit by the first spouse. Necessaries include food, clothing, and housing, as well as medical bills.

Need-based maintenance. A theory that a maintenance award should meet the recipient's needs, rather than be set at an amount reflecting what she contributed to a marriage or what she sacrificed.

No-fault divorce. The theory of divorce that allows a court to terminate the marital relationship without finding fault with one of the parties. In most states, a court has to find that the parties have irreconcilable differences (see entry) that justify terminating the marriage.

No-fault era. The period from approximately 1965 to 1980 during which most states adopted some form of no-fault divorce and made corresponding changes to their laws of maintenance and property distribution. The no-fault era is marked not only by changes to family law statutes, but by rapidly changing norms with regard to gender equality and sexuality.

Nonintervention doctrine. A doctrine, related to and often coterminous with marital privacy, that discourages courts from interfering with marital relationships or parent-child relationships.

Opportunity costs. In the maintenance context, those costs associated with one spouse having foregone opportunities for more lucrative paid work because of the labor she was performing for the family.

Parental autonomy. The deference courts show to parental decision making on behalf of children.

Parenting plan. An agreement between parents living apart about the care and custody of their children. The terminology represents an attempt to reduce the feeling of winners and losers in custody determinations and to increase the sense of collaboration between parents.

Parental rights. Those rights parents enjoy, both constitutional, statutory, and common law, to make decisions on behalf of and rear their children in a manner that they choose.

Percentage of income formula. One of the two primary child support formulas used by courts to determine child support amounts. The percentage of income formula determines an obligor's payments based on percentages of his income that vary according to the number of children (i.e., 20% for one child, 28% for two children).

Plural marriage. Marriage to more than one person at a time.

Polygamy. Plural marriage. As practiced in this country, polygamy has meant the marriage of one man and several wives — sometimes termed polygyny to distinguish it from polyandry (one woman married to more than one man). Polygamy is illegal in all states.

Rehabilitation-based maintenance. A maintenance award designed to provide the recipient with what she needs to rehabilitate herself as a market worker so that she can earn an appropriate level of income.

Role specialization. The practice among many married couples of dividing joint marital responsibilities so that each party specializes in particular roles. *See also* marital roles.

Second-parent adoption. The legal recognition of a second parent when a child already has one parent of the same gender as the parent who is adopting.

Separation from bed and board. Historically, the support that a husband owed a wife if the couple remained married but no longer lived in the same home.

Sperm donor. A man who provides sperm for the purpose of allowing another person or persons to fertilize an egg and bring a child to term. Donors who go through sperm banks are compensated and are relieved of all parental rights and responsibility for any child conceived. Some sperm donors provide sperm for friends or acquaintances, and they may or may not be relieved of parental rights and responsibilities.

Spousal evidentiary privileges. There are two spousal evidentiary privileges. The first, the spousal communication privilege, treats as confidential any communication between spouses said in private. The second, the adverse testimony privilege, allows a spouse not to testify against his or her spouse as to knowledge of events. Traditionally, either spouse could assert the testimonial privilege, meaning that either spouse could keep the other from testifying if he or she so desired. Today, in most states and as a matter of federal law, the testifying spouse holds the privilege, meaning that she can testify if she wants to, but she does not have to. Either party may still assert the confidential communications privilege.

Spousal tort law immunity. A doctrine prohibiting spouses from suing each other in tort. The doctrine has been eliminated in all states for intentional physical torts and in most states for physical torts based on negligence. States are mixed on the degree to which they entertain suits between spouses based on emotional harm.

Surrogate mother. A woman who carries a child to term intending to relinquish any parental rights or responsibilities she may have for the child to another person or persons who wish to parent the child.

Tender years doctrine. A child custody doctrine creating a presumption that mothers are the preferred custodians of young children. No state currently follows the tender years doctrine and its explicit gender preference is presumed to be unconstitutional.

Termination of parental rights. The formal elimination of all rights and responsibilities that a parent may have to his child. Voluntary termination can occur when a child is placed for adoption. Involuntary termination proceedings are instituted by the state after there has been a determination that the existing parent-child relationship poses a grave danger to the child that the state cannot reasonably remedy.

Uniform Marriage and Divorce Act. A model law published to give state legislatures guidance when drafting family codes and to provide consistency across states for the laws of divorce, marital property distribution, maintenance, and custody.

Uniform Parentage Act. A model law published to give state legislatures guidance when drafting family codes and to provide consistency across states for legal standards used in determining parenthood, particularly fatherhood.

Unilateral divorce. Divorce proceedings that can be instituted and obtained by one party to the marriage even if the other party does not wish to end the marriage. No-fault divorces can be unilateral, although often the party wanting a divorce has to wait longer than he or she would if his or her spouse agreed to the divorce.

Visitation. The legal right to spend time with a child. Visitation is presumptively appropriate for all parents whether or not they have broader custodial rights (*see* custody). In recent years visitation has sometimes been awarded to nonlegal parents. In certain states, some categories of nonlegal parents (grandparents and stepparents) have statutory rights to visitation.

Index